# CATALOG OF CHAMBER MUSIC
# FOR WIND INSTRUMENTS

Da Capo Press Music Reprint Series

GENERAL EDITOR

FREDERICK FREEDMAN

VASSAR COLLEGE

# CATALOG OF CHAMBER MUSIC FOR WIND INSTRUMENTS

## by Sanford M. Helm

*revised printing*

𝄞 DA CAPO PRESS · NEW YORK · 1969

# DEDICATED

To Julane and Janet, who nearly succeeded in completely interrupting this work, and to Jane, who with utmost patience restrained them from doing so.

A Da Capo Press Reprint Edition

This Da Capo Press edition is a revised and corrected printing of Sanford M. Helm's *Catalog of Chamber Music for Wind Instruments,* originally published in Ann Arbor, Michigan, in 1952, as Publication No. 1 of the National Association of College Wind and Percussion Instrument Instructors. It is reprinted by special arrangement with Sanford M. Helm.

*Library of Congress Catalog Card Number 70-86597*

Published by Da Capo Press
A Division of Plenum Publishing Corporation
227 West 17th Street
New York, N. Y. 10011

Printed in the United States of America

## TABLE OF CONTENTS

PREFACE

When in the Fall of 1951 the newly formed National Association of College Wind and Percussion Instrument Instructors requested that I prepare this catalog for publication, it was with considerable pleasure that I put aside all else and turned to the task. In 1945-1946 some of this material was prepared in typewritten copy, its purpose being intended to serve in what I felt was a pressing need, but because the script was not printed the inevitable result was that its use was limited to patrons of the University of Michigan library. Evidently the same need for similar catalogs was felt elsewhere also; a few such lists with limited coverage have since that time received some general distribution, and it is both interesting and satisfying to see in their prefaces an echo of the opening statements I made in my 1946 preface--

> "The need has been recognized, among those who play and teach wind instruments, for a catalog devoted to chamber music which includes winds...."

That these specialized catalogs materialize seems to be a signal that wind instrument music in this country is taking its place along side, not below, the position so long enjoyed by that for strings. As one searches through various bibliographical works, he cannot escape the observation that the works for winds are so often merely mentioned in passing, if at all, as incidental music. This situation could be taken as a slight on the profession, but it might also serve as a warning that in so many instances our reportoire is interspersed with stuff which cannot begin to compete with the quality of music for other performing groups. Due to the Band being a basic medium of Music Education, to the great popularity and stimulus of jazz with its emphasis on winds, to the general advancement of good music, and to many other forces, thousands of wind players are being produced. If playing an instrument is to be one of the approaches to the musical art, then the whole system is a farce if these players have little great music to approach. Therefore it is urgent that wind players individually or collectively seek out good music, and encourage new composition by good composers. It does not fall within the jurisdiction of this book to make these decisions as to worth; as a catalog it serves only to list the works.

What Music is Included:--Chamber music for 3 to 12 instruments (and some of slightly larger size) which employs at least one wind instrument. The primary aim has been to list chamber music as such, not including the quantity of teaching material that serves so well for that purpose alone. Of course this is a fine line to draw and in some cases, to be sure, an arbitrary one. In instances where there is a limited reportoire for a particular combination, it seemed advisable to have at least a representative listing. Most of the items are original compositions, although many are by necessity editions of the originals, and even some arrangements and transcriptions seemed to be appropriate.

Editions and Arrangements. These terms are used so loosely, even by some publishers, that clarification is in order. There are at least two kinds of editors of music. The first of these presents a composition which is the product of considerable study, including a review of the original manuscripts and original notation, sometimes necessitating transcription of old notation into modern, and realization of a figured bass line for keyboard within the style of the period. Again, the term editor may mean merely that a few articulations of staccato and phrase were added. Generally, an edition of music written before 1750 implies a real task of editing, and that is not to say music written after that time does not require it. The term "arrangement" may indicate anything from a faithful re-scoring to the extreme of being an almost completely new work. The scoring for obsolete instruments, the desire for different sonority, the need for a repertoire now non-existent, and the expedience of simplification, are the most frequent reasons for arrangements.

Editions of Baroque Music.    The flexibility of the music of the Baroque period (c. 1580-1750) presents a problem in edition.    For example, a Solo Sonata will have originally been written on two staves for a melody instrument and Continuo (Figured Bass), but it would have been performed by the melody instrument, perhaps a stringed or other bass playing the Continuo, and a keyboard instrument whose player improvised the harmonic structure from the Figured Bass.    Therefore three instruments play from two lines of music.    Likewise, a Trio-Sonata of three musical lines (two melody lines and Figured Bass) was performed by two melody instruments, a bass instrument, and keyboard.

Several things can be altered in modern editions of this music:    (1) the cello or bass instrument may be omitted, (2) one of the melody lines can be incorporated into the keyboard realization of the Figured Bass, so that what was originally a Trio-Sonata will emerge as a duo, (3) the keyboard realization can be omitted, thus what was a Trio-Sonata for two melody instruments, cello, and keyboard, will become simply a trio for three instruments.

The Baroque period, unlike the Nineteenth Century, many times did not conceive its music as being written particularly for a specific instrument; instead, so often the melody line or lines of a piece are playable equally well by violin, flute, oboe, recorder, or any combination of these, e. g. :*

| Written for | Playable as | | |
|---|---|---|---|
| | 2 Insts. | 3 Insts. | 4 Insts. |
| Melody line, FigBs (Solo Sonata) | Mel. Inst. , Pf or M el. Inst. , Vc | Mel. Inst. , Pf, Vc | |
| 2 Mel. lines, FigBs (Trio-Sonata) | Mel. Inst. , Pf | 2 Mel. Insts. , Pf or 2 Mel. Insts. , Vc | 2Mel. Insts. , Pf, Vc |

Use of the Catalog.    The material of the 1946 catalog was listed according to composer alphabetically.    It was thought that the information would be more readily usable if it were organized according to performing unit in this edition, and in order to retain the advantages of the alphabetical listing there is an index by composer.    A glance at the Table of Contents will reveal the scheme of classifying the performance unit.    When there was an alternative in performance unit, the larger size was taken, and usually there is a cross reference.    Also there is usually a cross reference where there are substitutions in the instrumentation.

Consequently each entry, used in conjunction with the Index, gives some or all of the following information in this order--

| Information | Symbols |
|---|---|
| 1. Name of composer. . . . . . . . . . . . . . . . . . | Always in CAPITALS |
| 2. Index:   full name. | |
| 3. Index:   dates of birth and death (and thus the style period). | |
| 4. Index:   other works by this man. | |
| 5. Name of composition. | |

---

*For abbreviations of instruments, see key to Abbreviations and Symbols.

| Information | (cont.) | Symbols |
|---|---|---|

6.  Key . . . . . . . . . . . . . . . . . . . . given:"--G" (G major)
                                                 "--g" ( g minor )

7.  Opus number. . . . . . . . . . . . . . . . . Op

8.  Date of composition. . . . . . . . . . . . . in (     ) following Op.

9.  Instrumentation, or peculiarities of instrumentation . . Each part separated by comma,
                                                 substitute insts. as (  ).

10. Editor or arranger.  . . . . . . . . . . . . Ed: or Arr:

11. Primary or original publisher, and date of
                  publication . . . . . . . . B&H(1910);

12. Availability at U. S. dealer. . . . . . . . . . . . . .      ; AMP
    (not always same edition as #11).

---

Example--

        5 INSTS. : including 1 Wind & Pf(Keyboard, etc. )

Ob, 3 Str, Pf(Hp)*

DOE    2 Quint--C, g; Op 45, 47 (1889).   Vl(Ob, Va), Va, Vc; uses Hp.
                  Ed: Schmidt.  . . . . . . . . . . . . . B&H(1896); AMP

---

The two pieces are by Doe, and according to the Index he is John Doe (1830-1895) and therefore likely a composer in the Romantic Style.   The first quintet is in C major, Opus 45, the second is in g minor (small letter "g"), Opus 47; both were written in 1889.   The instrumentation is for Oboe, Violin (with another Oboe or a Viola as substitute), Viola, Cello, and it calls for Harp rather than Piano.   Both were edited by Schmidt for Breitkopf and Hartel who published them in 1896; Associated Music Publishers generally carries these two items in stock.

Publishers.   In listing publishers, no attempt has been made to mention all or numerous publishers or dealers of any one work, purely as a space saving device.   The aim has been to impartially suggest where the music might be available, rather than to prepare a catalog of publication dates.   It is not to be presumed that all music listed is available from the publisher mentioned.   Many of these compositions are now out of print, but have nevertheless been listed for historical reasons and for information on reportoire. A key to publishers has been employed, the abbreviations of which are under the section devoted to publishers in the Appendix.   When the dotted line extends to the margin at the right, either the work is in manuscript, or the publisher is not known to me.

Coda.   A statement to the effect that the following catalog is a complete coverage would be sheer fantasy, although every effort has been made to make it be as complete as is possible with the materials available.   A work such as this is never finished because the musical art does not stand still.   So as it becomes undone I would be grateful for any notice of error, omission, or injustice which may be present.   Likewise I will be glad to answer any request for further information if I have it or can obtain it.

I am already indebted to several persons for their assistance and encouragement: first of all to the National Association of College Wind Instrument and Percussion Instructors and their President,   Prof. William Stubbins of the University of Michigan,   through whose organization a vehicle has been established for the promotion of Wind Instrument music;   several publisher's representatives who responded beyond the call of duty, Max Winkler of Belwin, K. E. Cummings of Boston Music, Merle Montgomery of C. Fischer,

---

*See pages devoted to Abbreviations in Appendix.

# PREFACE

Justin Burston of Keynote (Baxter-Northrup), Robert E. Teck of Mills, Alan Langenus of Presser, E. C. Schirmer, Benjamin Grasso of G. Schirmer, and numerous others who so kindly replied to my inquiries; Mrs. Rafael Druian, former librarian at Curtis Institute; Mrs. James Crane, librarian; several who have loaned personal material, Professor Russell Howland of Fresno, Simeon Bellison of New York, and my Ann Arbor colleagues Professor Theodore Heger of the Department of Music Literature, and James Salmon, Percussion Instructor; and to Dean E. V. Moore who was quick to offer certain facilities of the University of Michigan School of Music.

Sanford M. Helm
Ann Arbor, Michigan
March, 1952

# THREE INSTRUMENTS

## 3 INSTS.: including 1 Wind

### Fl, Vl, Va

AHLGRIMM  Divertimento--D . . . . . . . . . . . . . . . . . . Lienau(1938)
AMBROSIUS  Trio, Op 58 . . . . . . . . . . . . . . . . Author publ. (Leipzig, 1926)
BECHERT  Serenade--D, Op 4 . . . . . . . . . . . . . . Tischer & J(1933)
BEETHOVEN  Serenade--D, Op 25 (c1797) . . . . . . . . B&H(1864); AMP, Peters
BRUGGEMANN, [K?]  Trio--D . . . . . . . . . . . . . . Litolff(1937); Andraud
DAVID, J.N.  Trio, Op 30 . . . . . . . . . . . . . . . . . B&H(1942)
GABRIELSKI  Trio--A, Op 45 . . . . . . . . . . . . . . . . . . . . . . . .
GILSE  Trio--f# mi . . . . . . . . . . . . . . . . . . . . Alsbach(1931)
JEMNITZ Trio, Op 19 . . . . . . . . . . . . . . . . . . Zimmerman(1924)
JUNGEMANN  Trio-Suite--a mi, Op 21 . . . . . . . . . Ries & Erler(1871)
KUHN  Frohsinn--G . . . . . . . . . . . . . . . . . . . . . "       "    (1934)
MARTEAU, H.  Terzetto--D, Op 32 . . . . . . . . . . . . Simrock(1924); AMP
MOSER, RUD.  Divertimento, Op 48 #1 . . . . . . . . . . Vogel(1937)
PHILIPP  Serenade--d mi, Op 23 . . . . . . . . . . . . . Böhm(1932)
PORTER  Little Suite (1928) . . . . . . . . . . . . . . . . . . . . . . . .
REGER  Serenade--D, Op 77a . . . . . . . . . . . . . . Bote & Bock(1904)
        Serenade--G, Op 141a . . . . . . . . . . . . . Peters(1915); McG & M
REUSS  Trio--G, Op 61 . . . . . . . . . . . . . . . . . V. f. Musik-Kultur(1935)
ROSENBERG  Trio . . . . . . . . . . . . . . . . . . . Hansen(1930)
SCHADEWITZ  Serenade--G, Op 49 . . . . . . . . . . . Grosch(1942)
WEBER, LUDW.  Serenade--D . . . . . . . . . . . . . . Zimmerman(1927)
ZOELLER  Suite . . . . . . . . . . . . . . . . . . . . . Laudy(1891)

### Fl, Vl, Vc

AGERSNAP  Interludium . . . . . . . . . . . . . . . . Edit. Dania(1936); McG & M
HANSEN, EMIL  Trio--d mi, Op 13 . . . . . . . . . . . Zimmerman(1910)
HAYDN  6 Trios, Op 100.  Ed: Dittrich . . . . . . . . . Zimmerman(1926); Andraud
        3 Divertimenti--D, C, D.  Ed: Egidi . . . . . . . Vieweg(1936); Andraud
MOZART  Wiener Serenaden.  Ob or Cl for Fl.  Ed: Hoffman.. Kallmeyer(1943)
        *Drei leichte Trios--G, D, F; K Anh 229 . . . . . . Andre(1893)
PLEYEL  3 Trios--G, C, D; Op 73 . . . . . . . . . . . . . "     (1873)
REICHA  18 Var. & Fantasy on Th. of Mozart--G, Op 51 . . . B&H
WALCKIERS  Trio--D, Op 35 . . . . . . . . . . . . . . . Hamelle(c1850)

### Fl, 2 Misc. Str

AMBROSIUS  3 Preludes & Fugue.  Fl, 2Vl . . . . . . . . Litolff(1935)
KOTSCHETOW  Concertino, Op 4.  Fl, 2Vl . . . . . . . . UE(1929); Andraud
LANGE, G. FR.  Ein Heiteres Trio.  Fl, Vl, Cb . . . . . . . Erdmann(1881)
ROUSSEL  Trio--F, Op 40.  Fl, Va, Vc . . . . . . . . . . Durand(1930); E-V
SCHULHOFF  Concertino (1925).  Fl, Va, Cb . . . . . . . UE(1927)
STRINGFIELD  Ole Swimmin' Hole (1924).  Fl, Va, Vc . . . . . . . . . . . . .
TAUDOU  Trio--G, Op 1.  Fl, Va, Vc . . . . . . . . . . . Costallat(1877)

---

*Evidently not the 5 Trio Divertimenti K. Anh. 229, which are all in Bb.

## Ob, 2 Str

BALORRE   Trio--c mi.   With Va, Vc . . . . . . . . . . . Hamelle(1899); Andraud
HONEGGER   Choral.   With Vl, Vc . . . . . . . . . . . Hansen(c1935)
KOTSCHAU   Divertimento #2--e mi, Op 12b.   Ob(Fl), Va, Vc.   . Zimmerman(1932); B-N

## Cl, 2 Str

BECKERATH   Musik--D.    Cl, Vl(Fl, Ob), Vc(Bn) . . . . . . Litolff(1938)
BLUMER   Trio--d mi, Op 55.   With Vl, Vc. . . . . . . . Simrock(1928); AMP
BUSCH, ADOLF   German Dance, Op 26a.   With Vl, Vc . . . B&H(1926); Andraud
HEIDRICH   Trio--a mi, Op 33.   With Va, Vc . . . . . . . . Schmidt(1911); Andraud
HEROLD   Serenade--Bb.   With Va, Vc . . . . . . . . . .     "    (1886);     "
JUON   Divertimento--D, Op 34.   With 2 Va . . . . . . . Lienau(1927); ECSch
NERUDA, FRANZ   Mus. Märchen--Bb, Op 31.   With Va, Vc. . Hansen(c1878)
WOHLFAHRT   Trios für junge, 13 pcs, Op 191.   With Vl, Va. . R Forberg(1888)

## Misc: 1 Wind, 2 Str

BENTZON   Symfonisk Trio, Op 18.   Vl, Hn, Cb . . . . . . Kistner & S(1931)
FLAMENT   Fantaisie for Bn.   Bn, Vl, Vc . . . . . . . . . Buffet-Crampon(1922)
HAYDN   Divertimento (1767).   Hn, Vl, Vc . . . . . . . . . . . . . .
ROTERS   Trio, Op 26b.   Sx(Cl), Vl, Vc . . . . . . . . . Simrock(1926)
STICH   20 Trios.   Hn, Strs . . . . . . . . . . . . . . . . .

## 3 INSTS.: including 1 Wind & Pf(Keyboard, etc.)*

## Fl, Vl, Pf(Hp)

AMBROSIUS   Little Suite, Op 11 [?] . . . . . . . . . . . Zimmerman(1922)
BACH, FRIEDR.   Trio--C. Ed: Schunemann. . . . . . . . . Kistner & S(1920)
            Sonate.   Fl, Vl(Ob), Pf . . . . . . . . . Andraud
BACH, J. S.   Sonate--G.   Ed: numerous. . . . . . . . . . Durand; Andraud, IMC
BACH, K. P. E.   Trio--Bb.   Ed: Lorenz, Tschierpe . . . . Zimmerman(1928)
            Trio, 2nd Sonate . . . . . . . . . . . . Andraud
BACH, W. FR.   Sonata . . . . . . . . . . . . . . . . . . Peters; McG & M
BECKERATH   Sonatine--Eb . . . . . . . . . . . . . . . . Moeck(1939)
BOISDEFFRE   Serenade, Op 85 . . . . . . . . . . . . . . Hamelle; Andraud
BROD   Trio, Op 15 . . . . . . . . . . . . . . . . . . . . Noël
        Trio, Op 23.   Vl, Fl(Ob), Pf . . . . . . . . . . . .
COERNE   Trio, Op 139.   Fl, Vl, Hp . . . . . . . . . . . .
CORTICELLI   Divertimento pastorale, Op 64 . . . . . . . Ricordi(c1840)
CUI   5 Little Duets, Op 56 . . . . . . . . . . . . . . . Balaiev(1897)
FRANCAIX   Musique de Cour . . . . . . . . . . . . . . . Schott(1938); AMP
GAUBERT   Antiques Medallions . . . . . . . . . . . . . Andraud
GENIN, P. A.   Trio--a mi, Op 9 . . . . . . . . . . . . . . Costallat(1869)
GLUCK   Sonate--g mi . . . . . . . . . . . . . . . . . . Eschig(c1913)

---

*See remarks in Preface concerning the instrumentation of editions of Solo Sonatas and
  Trio Sonatas from the Baroque Era.

## Fl, Vl, Pf(Hp) cont.

GOOSENS  Suite, Op 6.   Fl, Vl, Hp(Pf) . . . . . . . . . . Chester(1917); Andraud
GUERRINI  Nocturne . . . . . . . . . . . . . . . Andraud
HANDEL   Kleine Ka Music um Handel  .  Ed: Heydt. . . . . . Böhm(1943)
HODGE  3 Sketches (1936) . . . . . . . . . . . . . . Chester(1937)
IBERT   Aria.   Fl, Vl(Cl), Pf. . . . . . . . . . . . . Andraud
        2 Interludes.   With Pf or Hp . . . . . . . . . . Andraud
MARTINU  Madrigal Sonata . . . . . . . . . . . . . . AMP
MEL-BONIS  Suite--e mi. . . . . . . . . . . . . Eschig(1898); Andraud
MIGOT  Le Livre de Danceries . . . . . . . . . . . M Baron
POPP  6 Jugend Trios, Op 505 . . . . . . . . . . . Litoloff(1901)
RABAUD   Andante et Scherzetto--G, Op 8 . . . . . . . Heugel(1899); Merc
STAMITZ  Trio--G, Op 14 #1.  Ed: Upmeyer  . . . . . . . Nagel(1928); Andraud
SUK  Bagatela (1917) . . . . . . . . . . . . . . . Hudebni Matice(1925);Andraud
TELEMANN   Trio Sonata--E,  #9 of Exercicii Musici* .  Ed: Ermeler, Päsler. . Nagel(1930)

## Fl, Va, Pf(Hp)

BAX   Elegiac Trio--G. With Hp. . . . . . . . . . . Chester(1920); MBaron
DEBUSSY  Sonata--g mi.  Fl(Vl), Va, Hp . . . . . . . . Durand(1916); E-V
DUBOIS  Terzettino.  Uses Hp.. . . . . . . . . . . Heugel(1904); MBaron
DURUFLE   Prelude recitatif et var., Op 3 . . . . . . . Durand(1929); E-V
FICHER  Sonata (1931) . . . . . . . . . . . . . .
GRAUPNER   Sonata--d mi.  Fl, Va d'amour(Va), Pf.  Ed: Kint . P Günther(1937)
HAHN  Romanesque--C (1910). . . . . . . . . . . . Heugel(1937); Merc
HEINICHEN   Trio--F.  Fl, Va d'amour(Va), Bs(Pf).   Ed: Kint . Günther(1941)
KAUFFMANN, LEO  Divertimento.  Fl, Gamba(Va), Pf. . . . . Schott(1938)
KOECHLIN  Suite, Op 55 . . . . . . . . . . . . . .
KUMMER  Trio--C, Op 75.  Fl, Va(Vl), Pf . . . . . . . . Andre(1867)
LOCATELLI  Trio--F.  Fl, Va d'amour(Va), Pf.  Ed: Kint . . . Günther(1941)
LOCKWOOD  Trio (1940).  Uses Hp. . . . . . . . . . .
ROHOZINSKI  Suite Breve, 4 mvts.  Uses Hp . . . . . . . Senart(1925)
SMIT  Trio.  Uses Hp. . . . . . . . . . . . . . . Senart(1929)
SOWERBY  Trio--e mi. . . . . . . . . . . . . . .
WEISMANN   Chamber Music--b mi, Op 86 . . . . . . . . W. Müller(Heidelberg, 1924)

## Fl, Vc, Pf(Hp, Organ)

_____  5 leichte Suiten aus dem Barock.   Ed: Dietz . . . . Schott(1937)
ANON. 17th C.   Suite--F.   Fl(Ob), Pf, Vc ad lib.   Ed: Bouvet. . Eschig; AMP
ALBINONI  Sonata--a mi.  Ed: Schäffler . . . . . . . . Nagel(1931)
BACH, FRIEDR.   Trio--D.   Ed: Schunemann . . . . . . . Kistner & S(1926)
BACH, J.S.   Sonata--g mi.  Fl, Vc, Pf obl . . . . . . . Nagel(Hannover); AMP
BARBO  2 Terzetti. . . . . . . . . . . . . . . . Ricordi
BATE  Trio . . . . . . . . . . . . . . . . . .
BLAVET   6 of 18 Sonatas for Fl, Bs(Pf & Vc), (1732) . . . . . Rudall & Carte
BONONCINI  Divertimento--c mi.  Fl(Ob), Vc, Pf.  Ed: Rodemann.  . Moeck; McG & M
BONVIN  Reminiscences for Orch., arr. as trio by composer . B&H; AMP
BUXTEHUDE   Trio Sonata--a mi, Op 1 #3.  Fl(Vl), Vc, Pf . . . Schott; AMP

*For others from this work see Telemann under Fl, Vc, Pf category.

Fl, Vc, Pf(Hp, Organ) cont.

COUPERIN, FRAN.   4 Royal Concerts: Preludes, Allemandes, Airs,
                            Echoes, Gigues, Minuets, etc. (1722-25)* . . Andraud
COUPERIN, LOUIS   2 Symphonies [Sinfonias].   Fl, Gamba(Vc), Pf.
                            Ed: Bouvet, Quittard . . . . . . . . Eschig(1908); AMP
CZERNY   Fantaisie concertante, Op 256 . . . . . . . . . . . . . . . . . . .
DAMASE   Trio.   Uses Hp . . . . . . . . . . . . . . . . Lemoine; E-V
DELLO JOIO   Trio . . . . . . . . . . . . . . . . . . . . . . CFisch
DEMERSSEMAN   Trios #2, 3, 5, 6, 7--b mi, ab mi, E, A, D. . . . . . . . Legouix(c1860)
DUPIN   Pieces Dialoguees.   Fl, Vc, Hp(Pf) . . . . . . . . . Durand(1923); E-V
DUSSEK   Trio--C, Op 21 . . . . . . . . . . . . . . . . . . B&H
             Trio--F, Op 65 . . . . . . . . . . . . . . . . . B&H
FARNABY   Suite from Fitzwm. Virginal Bk.   Uses Hp.   Arr: Hill . . . Riker(1934)
FARRENC   Trio--e mi, Op 46 . . . . . . . . . . . . . . . . Leduc(c1850)
FAUCONIER   Fantasie concertante .   Fl(Cl), Vc, Pf . . . . . . . . . Schott(1863)
FIOCCO   Sonate--g mi.   Fl(Ob), Pf, Vc ad lib.   Ed: Ruetz . . . . . . Schott(1939)
FISCHER   4 Suites.   Fl(Ob), Vc, Pf.   Ed: Woehl . . . . . . . Bärenreiter(1932)
FORESTIER   Trio--E, A; #1, 4 . . . . . . . . . . . . . . . . Legouix(c1860)
GAGNAIRE   Resurrection--G . . . . . . . . . . . . Author publ. (Bordeaux)
GARIBOLDI   Elegie & Scherzo, Op 180 . . . . . . . . . . . Lafleur(1885)
GAUBERT   3 Water Colors (1915) . . . . . . . . . . Bornemann(Paris, 1921); Andraud
GOOSENS   5 Impressions of a Holiday, Op 7 (1914) . . . . . . Chester(1916); MBaron
GRIMM, C.H.   4 Stencils . . . . . . . . . . . . . . . . . . . . . . . .
HANDEL   15 [i.e. 16] Chamber Sonatas, Op 1.   1 Inst(Fl, Vl, Ob), FigBs(Pf & Vc).
                  Ed: Seiffert . . . . . . . . . . . . . B&H; AMP
        Nr 1.  Op 1#1a--e, Fl     Nr 6.  Op 1#5--G, Fl     Nr 12.  Op 1#11--F, Fl
        Nr 2.  Op  #1b--e, Fl     Nr 7.  Op  #6--g, Ob     Nr 13.  Op  #12--F, Vl
        Nr 3.  Op  #2 --g, Fl     Nr 8.  Op  #7--C, Fl     Nr 14.  Op  #13--D, Vl
        Nr 4.  Op  #3 --A, Vl     Nr 9.  Op  #8--c, Ob     Nr 15.  Op  #14--A, Vl
        Nr 5.  Op  #4 --a, Fl     Nr 10. Op  #9--b, Fl     Nr 16.  Op  #15--E, Vl
                                  Nr 11. Op  #10--g, Vl

        3 Hallenser Sonaten--a, e, b; B&H Nr 17-19 (Halle, 1710).
              For Fl, FigBs(Pf&Vc).   Ed: Seiffert . . . . . . . B&H; AMP
          Chamber Sonata #22--D.   Ed: Seiffert . . . . . . . . . . B&H(1938); AMP
          4 Sonatas for Recorder--g, a, C, F.   Ed: Woehl . . . . . . Peters
          3 Sonatas--e, G, b.   Ed: Woehl . . . . . . . . . . . . Peters
HASSE   Suite--a mi, Op 36a.   Fl, Pf, Vc ad lib (not a Baroque pc.). . . Litolff(1934)
HAYDN   3 Trios--F, D, G; #29, 30, 31 (c1790). (orig. for strs.). . . . B&H; AMP, MBaron
             Trios--F,   G; #29,   31          (substitute insts.). . . . C-B
HILL, ALF.   Miniature Trio #2--C.   Fl(Cl, Ob), Vc(Bn), Pf . . . . . . G Sch(1928)
HILLEMACHER, PAUL & LUCIEN   Elegie . . . . . . . . . . . . Leduc(c1900)
HUMMEL   Sonate--Bb, Op 2#1 . . . . . . . . . . . . . . . . . . . .
             Adagio, Varns. & Rondo on a Russian Th., Op 78 . . . . . . . .
HÜNTEN   Trio--d mi, Op 91b . . . . . . . . . . . . . . . . Schott
KALBRENNER   Trio--Bb, Op 39 . . . . . . . . . . . . . . . B&H
KONINK   2 leichte Son. --d mi, g mi.   Ed: Friedrich . . . . . . . Schott(1937)
             Trio Sonatas--F, d mi, F; Nr 7, 9, 10.   Ed: Friedrich . . Moeck(1939); McG & M
KREUTZER, KONR.   2 Trios--Bb, G; Op 23 . . . . . . . . . . . . Simrock
KRONKE   Suite Italienne--F, Op 186.   Uses Hp . . . . . . . . . Zimmerman(1924)
KUHLAU   Trio, Op 119 . . . . . . . . . . . . . . . . . . . MBaron
LAJTHA   Trio--Eb.   Uses Hp . . . . . . . . . . . . . . . . Rozsavolgyi(1937)

---

*Originally on 2 staves, sometimes 3.   Couperin recommended Vl(Ob, Viol) & Bn for performance.

## Fl,   Vc,   Pf(Hp, Organ) cont.

LECLAIR   Trio Sonata.   Vc or Va.    Ed: Bouvet . . . . . . Eschig: AMP
LEDUC   Trio, Op 66.   Vc or Bn. . . . . . . . . . . . Leduc
LEMACHER   Volkslieder Suite.   Vc or Va or Gamba . . . . Litolff(1944)
LIEBIG   2 Trio Satze--D, A;  Op 7, 8. . . . . . . . . . . B&H(1890)
LOTTI   Sonate--G.   Vc or Gamba.   Ed: Döbereiner. . . . Zimmerman(1928); Andraud
MACFARREN   Romance & Allegro . . . . . . . . . . . . Rudall(1883)
MARTINU   Trio (1944) . . . . . . . . . . . . . . . . AMP
MASCITTI   Sonate--g mi.   Ed: Peyrot & Rebuffat. . . . . . Senart(1934)
MAYSEDER   Trio--G, Op 59 . . . . . . . . . . . . . . Augener(1881)
MIGOT   Concert.   Hp or Pf. . . . . . . . . . . . . . Leduc(1931); MBaron
PEPUSCH   Sonatas--C, d mi, G, F, Bb, Bb, G, d mi;  Nr 1-8.
              Fl(Ob), Gamba(Vc), Pf.   Ed: Dancker-Langer . . Moeck(1939)
          ditto . . . . . . . . Nr 1, 2. . . . . . . . McG & M
          ditto . . . . . . . . Nr 1-6. . . . . . . . Schott
PIERNE, GABR.   Serenade, Op 7 . . . . . . . . . . . Leduc
              Sonata da Camera--C, Op 48 . . . . . . Durand(1928); E-V
RAMEAU   5 Concert Pcs. , Set I (1712).   Ed: Peyrot & Rebuffat . . Senart(1911)
REY   6 petits trios . . . . . . . . . . . . . . . . . Author publ. (Paris, 1877)
RICHTER   Sonata da Camera--A.   Ed: Riemann, Collegium Mus. #18. . B&H; AMP
          Sonata--G.   Ed: Zirnbauer. . . . . . . . . . Schott(1941)
          Trio--g mi.   Ed: Riemann, D. T. B.   Bd. 28 . . . B&H(1915)
RIEGGER   Divertissement, Op 15 (1933).   Uses Hp . . . . . . . . . .
RIES   Trio--Eb, Op 63 (1825). . . . . . . . . . . . . . . . . . .
SKROUP   Trio, Op 28 . . . . . . . . . . . . . . . . Peters(1847)
         Trio--G, Op 30 . . . . . . . . . . . . . . . Peters(1849)
SPEAIGHT   Lament and Caprice. . . . . . . . . . . . . . . . . . . .
SPOHR   Trio--a mi, Op 124 . . . . . . . . . . . . . . . Augener(1884)
TELEMANN   12 Methodische Sonaten (Hamburg, 1728-32).   Ed: Seiffert. . McG & M
          Sonata--b mi, Tafelmusik I#5(1733).   Ed: Seiffert. . . . B&H(1928); AMP
          "Esercizi Musici, " 12 Solo-& 12 Trio-Sonatas for various insts . . . . . .
          Sonatas--d mi, C; From Esercizi Musici.   Ed: Woehl . . Peters
          Chamber Sonata--D. . . . . . . . . . . . . . B&H; AMP
          Trio--F.   Fl, Gamba(Va, Vc), Pf.   Ed: Upmeyer. . . . Nagel(1937)
          Sonaten--Bb, c mi.   Ed: Seiffert . . . . . . . . . Kistner(1924)
          Sonata--C, from Getreuer Musikmeister(1728) . . . . . Peters
TERSCHAK   Trio--A, Op 22 . . . . . . . . . . . . . . J. Schuberth(1860)
TOESCHI   Trio--G.   Ed: Riemann, D. T. B. Bd. 28. . . . . B&H(1915)
VALENTINO   Sonata #9, 10.   Fl, Gamba(Vc), Pf.   Ed: Giesbert.Schott(1938)
VINCI   Sonate--D.   Ed: Wittaker. . . . . . . . . . . . OUP(1929)
VIVALDI   Pastorale--A, from Op 13#4.   Fl(Ob), Vc, Organ(Pf).
              Ed: Upmeyer. . . . . . . . . . . . . Nagel; AMP, IMC
WALCKIERS   Trio--d mi, Op 97. . . . . . . . . . . . . Costallat(c1860)
WEBER, C. M.   Trio--g mi, Op 63 (1819) . . . . . . . . Lienau(1869); IMC, MBaron
WERNER   Concertino . . . . . . . . . . . . . . . . Durand; E-V


## Fl, misc. , Pf(Hp)

HARTUNG   Trio-Serenade, Op 42.   Fl, Va d'amour, Hp. . . . P. Günther(1942)
HAYDN   Sonata.   Fl, Hp, Bs. . . . . . . . . . . . . . . . . .

## Fl, misc., Pf(Hp) cont.

MOZART    Concerto for Fl, Hp, Orch--C, K 299 (1778). Arr. for
                   Fl, Hp, Pf.  Ed: Salzedo, Cad. by Reinecke. Andraud
NERUDA, J.B.   Sonata--D.  Fl, Va d'amour, Pf.  Ed: Kint . .  P. Günther(1938)
ROGOWSKI   A Piece for Fl, Pf, Little Bells. . . . . . . . .  B. Gondanez(Paris)
TELEMANN   Trio--D.  Fl, Va d'amour, Pf.  Ed: Kint . . .  P. Günther

## Ob(EH), Vl, Pf

BACH, J.S.   Concerto--c mi. . . . . . . . . . . . . . .  B-N, IMC
            Concerto--d mi. . . . . . . . . . . . . . .  AMP
BECKERATH   Sonatine--Eb.  Fl(Ob), Vl, Pf. . . . . . . .  Moeck(1939)
BROD   Trio, Op 15.  Fl(Ob), Vl, Pf. . . . . . . . . .  Noël
       Trio, Op 23.  Fl(Ob), Vl, Pf. . . . . . . . . . . . . . . .
HANDEL   Sonata--Bb.  Ed: Hinnenthal. . . . . . . .  Bärenreiter(1935); McG & M
MIGOT   Le soir tombe. . . . . . . . . . . . . . . .  Senart(1918); B-N
TOVEY   Trio--d mi, Op 14.  Vl, EH, Pf. . . . . . . . .  Schott(1913)

## Ob, Va, Pf

BOHNE, R.   Serenade, Op 35.  Ob, Va(Vc), Pf. . . . . . .  B-N
EDELE   4 Songs Without Words, Op 2. . . . . . . . .  Simrock(1852)
HEINICHEN   Trio Sonata--c mi.  Ob(Fl), Gamba(Va), Pf . . .  Doblinger; AMP
KAUDER   Trio--d mi. . . . . . . . . . . . . . . .  UE(1924); B-N
KLUGHARDT   Trio, Op 28. . . . . . . . . . . . . .  Peters(1873)
KOTSCHAU   Divertimento.  Ob(Fl), Va, Pf. . . . . . . . . .
           Divertimento #2 . . . . . . . . . . . . . .  B-N
LOEFFLER   Rhapsody, La Cornemuse . . . . . . . . . .  GSch(1905)
          Rhapsody, l'Etang . . . . . . . . . . . .  GSch(1905)
RUTHARDT   Trio pastorale--G, Op 34. . . . . . . . . .  Kistner(1890)
WHITE   Nymph's Complaint for Death of her Fawn . . . . .  Stainer & Bell(1921)

## Ob, Vc, Pf(Organ)

ANON.   17th C.  Suite--F.  Fl(Ob), Pf, Vc ad lib.  Ed: Bouvet.  Eschig: AMP
AGNEL   Trio--D, Op 2.  Ob, Vc(Bn), Pf. . . . . . . . .  Costallat; B-N
BOHNE, R.   Serenade, Op 35.  Ob, Va(Vc), Pf. . . . . . .  B-N
BOISDEFFRE   Poeme pastoral--Eb, Op 87 . . . . . . . .  Hamelle
BONONCINI   Divertimento--c mi.  Fl(Ob), Gamba(Vc), Pf.
              Ed: Rodemann . . . . . . . . . . . . .  Moeck(1939); McG & M
DUBOIS   2 Pcs. in canonic form--F, A. . . . . . . . . .  Heugel(1900); MBaron
FIOCCO   Sonate--g mi.  Fl(Ob), Pf, Vc ad lib.  Ed: Ruetz. . .  Schott(1939)
FISCHER   4 Suites.  Fl(Ob), Vc, Pf.  Ed: Woehl. . . . . .  Bärenreiter(1932)
HANDEL   From 15 Chamber Sonatas, Op 1, see under <u>Fl, Vc, Pf</u> category.
       Chamber Sonatas #7, 9--g mi, c mi; Op 1#6, 8. . . .  B&H; AMP
       Chamber Sonata #5--a mi, Op 1#4.  Ob(Fl), Vc, Pf.
               Ed: Seiffert . . . . . . . .  B&H(1920)
       Chamber Sonata #9--c mi, Op 1#8.  Ob, Pf, Vc(Bn).
               Ed: Seiffert . . . . . . . .  B&H(1915)
HILL, ALF.   Miniature Trio #2--C.  Fl(Ob, Cl), Vc(Bn), Pf. . .  GSch(1928)

Ob, Vc, Pf(Organ) cont.

PEPUSCH    Sonatas--C, d, G, F, Bb, Bb, G, d; Nr 1-8.  Fl(Ob), Vc, Pf.
      Ed: Dancker-Langer . . . . . . .    Moeck(1939)
    ditto, Nr 1, 2.  . . . . . . . . . . . . . . . .    McG & M
    ditto, Nr 1-6.  Ed: Giesbert . . . . . . . .    Schott
ROESGEN-CHAMPION   Pastorale--F. . . . . . . . . .    Senart(1932); B-N
TELEMANN   Sonata--g mi, Tafelmusik III#5.  Ed: Seiffert .    B&H(1931)
   Esercizi Musici, see Fl, Vc, Pf category.
   Sonata--c mi.  Ed: Hinnenthal . . . . . . .    B&H(1938)
VIVALDI   Pastorale--A, from Op 13#4.  Fl(Ob), Vc, Organ(Pf).
     Ed: Upmeyer. . . . . . . . . . .    Nagel; AMP, IMC
WEBER, EDM.   Terzetto--d mi, Op 27.  Organ or Pf. . . .    Bosworth(1884)


Cl, Vl, Pf(Hp)

BARTOK   Contrasts (1938) . . . . . . . . . . . . . . .    Boosey
BAUSSNERN   Serenade--Eb. . . . . . . . . . . . . . .    Simrock(1905); AMP
FANING   Allegro sostenuto. . . . . . . . . . . . . . .    Lafleur(1892)
KHACHATURIAN   Trio--Bb. . . . . . . . . . . . . .    Russ. Staats-V.(1935); IMC
KRENEK   Trio (1946) . . . . . . . . . . . . . . . . . . .
KÜHNE   3 Musical Pictures. . . . . . . . . . . . . .    Author publ. (London, 1882)
MASON   Pastorale, Op 8 (1909-12) . . . . . . . . .    Salabert(Paris, 1913)
MILHAUD   Suite. . . . . . . . . . . . . . . . . . . .    Deiss(1937); Andraud
MOLNAR   Serenade.  Uses Hp. . . . . . . . . . .    Rozsavolgyi(1911)
STRAVINSKY   l'histoire du soldat.  Arr. by composer. . . .    Chester(1920); Andraud
WALTHEW   Trio--c mi. . . . . . . . . . . . . . . .    Boosey(1897)


Cl, Va, Pf

AMBERG   Fantasiestücke, Op 12.  Va or Vc. . . . . . .    Hansen(1911)
BRUCH   8 Pcs., Op 83.  Va or Vc.  . . . . . . . . .    Simrock(1910); AMP
HOLLÄNDER   6 Characteristic Pcs. in Canon Form, Op 53 .    Lienau(1898); Andraud
JACOBSSON, JOHN   Tre Stycken. . . . . . . . . . .    Musikal. Konstfören(c1900)
MOZART   Trio--Eb, K 498 (1786). . . . . . . . . . .    B&H(1856, '70); AMP
   ditto  . . . . . . Ed: Adamowski . . . .    GSch
REHM   Divertimento--G.  . . . . . . . . . . . . . .    Ochsner(1934)
REINECKE   Trio--A, Op 264. . . . . . . . . . . . . .    Simrock(1903)
SCHUMANN, ROBT.   Marchenerzahlungen, 4 pcs. --Bb, g, G, Bb;
      Op 132 (1853) . . . . . . . .    B&H(1854); AMP
UHL   Kleines Konzert.  . . . . . . . . . . . . . .    Doblinger(1938)


Cl, Vc, Pf

AMBERG   Trio--Eb, Op 11. . . . . . . . . . . . . .    Hansen(1912)
    Fantasiestücke, Op 12.  Va or Vc. . . . . . .    Hansen(1911)
BEETHOVEN   Trio--Bb, Op 11 (1797-98). . . . . . . .    B&H(1867); AMP
    ditto . . . . . . . . . . . . . . . . .    GSch, Peters
    Trio--Eb, Op 38.  Arr. from Septet Op 20 by Beeth. . B&H(1864); AMP
BERGER, WILH.   Trio--g mi, Op 94. . . . . . . . . . .    Kahnt(1905); Andraud
BLANC   Trio--Bb, Op 23. . . . . . . . . . . . . . .    Costallat
BRAHMS   Trio--a mi, Op 114. . .  . . . . . . . . .    Simrock(1892); AMP, M Baron

Cl, Vc, Pf  cont.

BROOKS    Trio--Eb, Op 12. . . . . . . . . . . . . Woolhouse(1906)
BRUCH     8 Pcs. , Op 83.  Va or Vc.  . . . . . . . . Simrock(1910); AMP
CORTICELLI  3 Trios, Op 56, 60, 63. . . . . . . . . Ricordi(c1840)
FARRENC   Trio--Eb, Op 44. . . . . . . . . . . Leduc(c1865)
FAUCONIER  Fantasie concertante.  Fl(Cl), Vc, Pf. . . . . Schott(1863)
FRUHLING  Trio--a mi, Op 40. . . . . . . . . . Leuckart(1925)
GROVERMANN  Trio--b mi.  . . . . . . . . . . Sander(1940)
HARTMANN  Serenade in 3 mvts. --A, Op 24. . . . . . . Hansen(1878)
HILL, ALF.  Miniature Trio #1--F. . . . . . . . . . GSch(1927)
          Miniature Trio #2--C.  Fl(Ob, Cl), Vc(Bn), Pf. . . GSch(1928)
HUNTEN    Terzetto, Op 175. . . . . . . . . . Schott(1851)
d'INDY    Trio--Bb, Op 29 (1887) . . . . . . . . . . Hamelle(1887); IMC
IRELAND   Trio--d mi. . . . . . . . . . . . . . .
JUON      Trio Miniaturen.   Arr. from StrTrio Op 18#3, 7, 6 & Op 24#2. . Lienau(1941)
KAHN      Trio--g mi, Op 45. . . . . . . . . . . Lienau(1906)
KERR      Trio (1936). . . . . . . . . . . . . NME XIII#3(1941)
POTTER    3 Trios, Op 12.  Vl(Cl), Vc(Bn), Pf. . . . . . Simrock
RIES      Trio--g mi, Op 28 (1810). . . . . . . . . .
SKROUP    Trio--Eb, Op 2. . . . . . . . . . . . Hoffman(Prague, 1846)
VOLLWEILER   Trio on Italian Themes, Op 15. . . . . . . J. Schuberth(1846)
          Fantaisie on Russian Airs--d mi, Op 35. . . . Lienau(1870)
ZEMLINSKY  Trio--d mi, Op 3. . . . . . . . . . . . Simrock(1897); AMP


Hn, Vl, Pf(Hp) unless otherwise given.

BRAHMS    Trio--Eb, Op 40. . . . . . . . . . . Simrock(1868); AMP, IMC
KOECHLIN  Pcs. , Op 32. . . . . . . . . . . .
MAYSEDER  Trio--F, Op 41.  Uses Hp. . . . . . . . . . . .
MOZART    Quintet for Hn, StrQuar--Eb, K 407 arr. for Trio by Naumann. . B&H(1907)
NISLE     Trio--f mi. . . . . . . . . . . . . . B&H
RAFF      2 Romances, Op 182.  Hn, Vc, Pf. . . . . . . . . . .


Misc: 1 Wind, 1 Str, Pf(Hp)

BACKOFEN  Concertante--F, Op 7.  BassetHn, Vc, Hp. . . . . . . . . .
BODECKER  Sonata sopra La Monica.  Vl, Bn, Pf.  Ed: Seiffert. . Kistner(1936)
HINDEMITH  Trio, Op 47.  Va, Heckelphone(TenSx), Pf.  . . . Schott(1930); AMP
HOLBROOKE  Fairyland, Op 57.  Ob d'amour(Fl, Ob, Cl), Va, Pf. Chester; B-N, MBaron
KREJCI    Trio.  Cl, Cb, Pf. . . . . . . . . . . . . Vlastnim(Prague, 1937)
LACOMBE, PAUL  Dialogue sentimental.  Vl(Fl), Bn(Vc), Pf. . Heugel(1917)
RUDINGER  Divertimento--g mi, Op 75.  Va(Cl), TenSx(BsCl, Vc), Pf. . . Böhm(1930)


                    3 INSTS. : including 2 Winds

2 Fl, 1 Str

ARDEVOL   2nd Sonata from Dos Sonatas a Tres.  With Va. . . Edit. Coop. ; SMPC
BACH, W. FR. E.  Trio--G.  With Va.  Ed: Ermeler. . . . Bärenreiter
FREDERICK THE GREAT.  Andante.  With Vl. . . . . . . Andraud

## 2 Fl, 1 Str cont.

HAYDN    London Trios #1-4--C, G, G, G.  With Vc.  Ed: Balet . .  Nagel; McG & M
        3 Trios--C, G, G; [London?].  With Vc.  Ed: Lenzewski.  Vieweg(1927)
RUST    Trio--D.  With Va d'amour.  Ed: Czach, in Erbe dt. Musik. Kallmeyer(1939)

## Misc. including 2 Winds

ARDEVOL    1st Sonata from Dos Sonatas a Tres.  Ob, Cl, Vc.   . .  Edit. Coop. ; SMPC
BECKERATH    Musik--D.  Vl(Fl, Ob), Cl, Vc(Bn). . . . . . . . .  Lifolff(1938)
BENTZON    Intermezzo.  Fl, Cl, Vl. . . . . . . . . . . . . . . . . . . . .
ETLER    Sonata.  Ob, Cl, Va. . . . . . . . . . . . . . . . . . . .  Valley
HENNESSY    Trio--Ab, Op 70.  Vl, Fl, Bn. . . . . . . . . . .  Eschig, Schott(1929)
HOLST    Terzetto, Op 44 (1925).  Fl, Ob, Va.  . . . . . . . . .  MBaron
KOCHER-KLEIN    Kleine Serenade, Op 26.  Fl, Ob(Vl), Vc. . . . .  Böhm(1928)
KOHS    Night Watch (1943).  Fl, Hn, Tymp. . . . . . . . . . . . . . .
KOUTZEN    Music (1940).  Sx, Bn, Vc. . . . . . . . . .  Broadcast; AMP
MALER    Sechs kleine Spielmusiken.  Vl, Fl(Ob, Vl), Ob(Cl) . . .  Schott(1931)
MARKEVITCH    Serenade.  Vl, Cl, Bn.  . . . . . . . . . .  Schott; AMP
McKAY    2 Mvts.  Cl, Bn, Cb.  . . . . . . . . . . . . . . .
REICHA    12 Trios.  2Hn, Vc.  . . . . . . . . . . . . . .
THOMPSON    Suite (1940).  Ob, Cl, Va. . . . . . . . . . . . .  ECSch
VILLA-LOBOS    Poeme de l'Enfant et de sa Mere.  Fl, Cl, Vc. . . . . . .
WECKMANN    2 Sonatas--a mi, C.   Cornettino(Vl), Vl, Bn(Tb, Gamba).
               Ed: Ilgner, in Erbe dt. Musik. . . . . .  Litolff(1942)
ZIMMERMAN    2 Trios--F, C.   Ob, Bn, Vc. . . . . . . . . .  Schmidt(1885)

## 3 INSTS. : including 2 Similar Winds & Pf(Keyboard, etc. )*

## 2 Fl, Pf(Hp)

ANDERSON    Allgo. Militaire, Op 48.   Orch or Pf. . . . . . . .  Zimmerman; B-N
BACH, J. C.    Divertissement for 2Fl, Orch.    Arr: M & L Moyse.  Andraud
BACH, K. P. E.    Trio Sonata--E.  Ed: Walther. . . . . . .  Zimmerman; B-N
BACH, W. FR.    3 Trios--D, D, a mi.  Ed: Seiffert. . . . . .  B&H(1934)
BENNETT    6 Souvenirs (1948). . . . . . . . . . . . . . . . . . . . . . .
BERLIOZ    Trio from Childhood of Christ, Op 25.   2Fl, Hp.
           Ed: Schuecker. . . . . . . . . . . . . .  B&H(1904); AMP, B-N
BOISMORTIER    2 Sonates--C, G. . . . . . . . . . . . . . .  B-N
BONONCINI    7 Suites.  2Fl(Ob), Pf.  Ed: Giesbert. . . . . .  Schott(1939)
BRICCIALDI    Duettino, Op 49. . . . . . . . . . . . . . . .  B-N
        Duo--D, Op 67. . . . . . . . . . . . . .  Schott(1853)
        Duo Brilliant--A, Op 130.  . . . . . . . .  Schott(1881); B-N
        Serenade, Op 137. . . . . . . . . . . . .  B-N
BURGHARDT    Trio Sonata--C, Op 42. . . . . . . . . .  Bärenreiter(1941)
         Partita brevis #2, Op 44.  . . . . . . .  Bärenreiter(1940)
CIMAROSA    Concerto for 2Fl, Orch--G.  Arr: M & L Moyse. . .  Andraud
CLINTON    Trios--Bb, A, F, G, g mi, Eb; Op 2, 3, 10, 33, 34, 35. . .  Ashdown
        Trios Ongarese--G; Op 11, 12. . . . . . . . . .  Ashdown
CORELLI    Gigue.  2Fl(Cl), Pf.  . . . . . . . . . . . . . .  MBaron
FASCH  Sonata a tre #1.  2Ob(Fl), Pf.   Ed: Schaffler. . . . . .  Nagel(1930); B-N
FESCH  3 Sonatas. . . . . . . . . . . . . . . . . . . .  Peters; McG & M

*See remarks in Preface on instrumentation of Baroque Trio-Sonata editions.

## 2 Fl, Pf(Hp) cont.

FÜRSTENAU  Rondo Brilliant, Op 102. . . . . . . . . . . . B-N
GAUBERT  Divertissement Grec.  Uses Hp. . . . . . . . . MBaron
GENIN, P. A.  Trio--a mi, Op 9.  Fl, Vl(Fl), Pf. . . . . . . Costallat(1869)
HAMMERSCHMIDT  Ballet & Canzone #2 in 3 pts.  2Fl(Ob), Pf.
        Ed: Moeck. . . . . . . . . . . McG & M
HANDEL  Trio Sonata--c mi, Op 2#1.  2Fl(Ob), Pf.  Ed: Seiffert. B&H(1903)
HERMAN  Rondo Turc; Tarantelle. . . . . . . . . . . . MBaron
KRONKE  Suite in olden style--a mi, Op 164. . . . . . . . Zimmerman(1922); B-N
KUHLAU  Trio--G, Op 119.  Ed: Kurth. . . . . . . . . . Simrock(1905); B-N
LE BEAU  Canon--e mi, Op 38.  2Fl(Ob, Cl), Pf. . . . . . . Schmidt(1895-97)
LECHTHALER  Freundliche Abendmusik.  Fl, Cl(Fl), Pf. . . . Böhm(1942)
LOCATELLI  Sonate--e mi. . . . . . . . . . . . . . . B-N
LOEILLET  2 Trio Sonatas--e mi, g mi.  Ed:  Beon . . . . Lemoine(1911)
MOUQUET  Divertissement Grec.  Pf or Hp. . . . . . . . B-N
QUANTZ  Sonata--D.  Ed: Fischer, Wittenbecher. . . . . . Forberg(1921)
   Andante from Sonata. . . . . . . . . . . . . C-B
SCHULTZ  Overture #1--F.  Ed: Moeck. . . . . . . . . McG & M
SOUSSMANN  Trio Concertant, Op 30. . . . . . . . . . . Richault
TELEMANN  Trio--D, Tafelmusik III.  Ed: Seiffert, in D. d. T. . B&H(1928)
   For other Tafelmusik see 2Fl, Vc, Pf category.
   Trio Sonata--C. . . . . . . . . . . . . . . . McG & M
TERSCHAK  Numerous duets for 2Fl, Pf. . . . . . . . . . . . . . .
TULOU  Trio--A, Op 83. . . . . . . . . . . . . . . . Schott


## 2 Ob, Pf

BODINUS  Sonata--Eb.  Ed: Fischer. . . . . . . . . . . Vieweg(1939)
BONONCINI  7 Suites.  2 Fl(Ob), Pf.  Ed: Giesbert. . . . . . Schott(1939)
FASCH  Sonata a tre #1.  2Ob(Fl), Pf.  Ed: Schaffler. . . . . Nagel(1930); B-N
HAMMERSCHMIDT  Ballet & Canzone #2 in 3 Pts.  2Fl(Ob), Pf. . Moeck; McG & M
HANDEL  Trio Sonata--c mi, Op 2#1.  2Fl(Ob), Pf. Ed: Seiffert . B&H(1903)
   3 Sonatas--d mi, Eb, D. . . . . . . . . . . . . IMC
LE BEAU  Canon--e mi, Op 38.  2Fl(Ob, Cl), Pf. . . . . . . Schmidt(1895)
ROMAN  Sonata. . . . . . . . . . . . . . . . . . . McG & M
STOELZEL  Sonata. . . . . . . . . . . . . . . . . . B-N


## Other Duos, Pf(Hp)

BEETHOVEN  Septet--Eb, Op 20.  Arr: 2Tb, Pf by Delisse . . . Millereau(1882)
    Sextet--Eb, Op 81b.  Arr: 2Hn, Pf by Kling . . . . Oertel(1884)
CORELLI  Gigue.  2Fl(Cl), Pf. . . . . . . . . . . . . MBaron
CURZON  Busybodies.  2Tt, Pf. . . . . . . . . . . . . Boosey
LE BEAU  Canon--e mi, Op 38.  2Fl(Ob, Cl), Pf. . . . . . . Schmidt(1895)
MIKULICZ  Romantisches Scherzo.  2Hn, Hp. . . . . . . . Fröhlich(1940)
MOZART  Trio for Cl, Va, Pf--Eb, K 498 (1786).  Arr: 2Cl, Pf.. MBaron
STÖHR  Trio--a mi, Op 53.  2Bn, Pf. . . . . . . . . . . Strache(Vienna, 1918)
UCCELLINI  2 Trio Sonatas--e mi, c mi; #16, 17.  2 Winds, Pf. . Ricordi(1907)
VIVALDI  Concerto--C.  Arr: 2Tt, Pf by Ghedini. . . . . . . IMC

## Fl, Ob(EH), Pf(Hpschd, Hp)

BACH, FRIEDR.   Sonate.   Fl, Vl(Ob), Pf. . . . . . . . . . . . . Andraud
BACH, J. C.   Divertissement for 2Fl, Orch.   Arr: Fl, Fl(Ob), Pf
                     by Moyse. . . . . . . . . . . . . Andraud
BACH, J. S.   Adagio.   Arr: Fl, Ob(Vl, Cl), Pf by Sarlit. . . . . . MBaron
CHRETIEN   Serenade sous Bois. . . . . . . . . . . . . . . . . . B-N
CIMAROSA   Concerto for 2Fl, Orch--G.   Arr: Fl, Fl(Ob), Pf  by Moyse . . Andraud
DAHLHOFF   Pan and the Nymphs.   Uses Hp. . . . . . . . . . Schmidt(1925); B-N
DEMERSSEMAN   Fantaisie Concertante, Op 36. . . . . . . . . B-N
DOUARD   3rd Concert Duo. . . . . . . . . . . . . . . . . . . B-N
          4th Concert Duo. . . . . . . . . . . . . . . . . . . B-N
FILLAUX-TIGER   Deux Pieces Pastorales. . . . . . . . . . . B-N
FUX   Sinfonia--F.   Ed: Kentner. . . . . . . . . . . . . . . Nagel(1938)
GAUBERT   Tarantelle. . . . . . . . . . . . . . . . . . . . . Andraud, B-N
GOEPFART   Trio--c mi, Op 74. . . . . . . . . . . . . . . . Schuberth(1898); B-N
GOOSENS   Pastorale and Harlequinade, Op 39 (1924). . . . . . Curwen(1925); B-N
HAMM   Dialogue.   Fl, Ob(Cl), Pf. . . . . . . . . . . . . . CFisch, B-N
HOLST   Fugal Concerto, Op 40#2.   Fl, Ob, Strs(Pf). . . . . . B-N
HONEGGER   Concerto da Camera.   Fl, EH, Strs(Pf). . . . . . McG & M
LACOMBE, PAUL   Serenade d'automne--G, Op 47. . . . . . . Hamelle; B-N
LANGEY   Gondolier and Nightingale, Op 49. . . . . . . . . . B-N
LECAIL   Pastorale. . . . . . . . . . . . . . . . . . . . . . B-N
LEROUX   Une Simple Idee. . . . . . . . . . . . . . . . . . . B-N
LOEILLET   2 Sonatas--c mi, d mi; Nr 5, 16.   Ed: Beon   . . . . Lemoine(1911)
        Trio Sonata--d mi, [Nr 15?]. . . . . . . . . . . . MusPr; Merc
        Trio Sonata--F. . . . . . . . . . . . . . . . . . Schott; AMP
MANCINI   Pastorale. . . . . . . . . . . . . . . . . . . . . B-N
MOZART   Fantasy for Mech. Organ--f mi, K 608 (1791).   Arr. . . B-N
MÜLLER, IWAN   Concertante, Op 23. . . . . . . . . . . . . B-N
PILLEVESTRE   Hero et Leandre.   Fl, Ob(EH), Pf. . . . . . . B-N
QUANTZ   Sonata--c mi.   Ed: Blumenthal. . . . . . . . . . . Zimmerman; B-N
SABON, ED.   Charite-Offertoire. . . . . . . . . . . . . . . Costallat; B-N
SABON, J. & DOUJON   Trio. . . . . . . . . . . . . . . . . . Durand(1865)
SMYTH   2 Interlinked French Folk Melodies. . . . . . . . . . OUP(1928); B-N
       Var. on Bonny Sweet Robin. . . . . . . . . . . . . OUP  ; B-N
TELEMANN   Trio Sonata--c mi, Exercicii Musici.
            Fl, Ob(Vl, Gamba), Pf.   Ed: Woehl. . . . . . . Peters(1938)
         Trio Sonata--C, Exercicii Musici.  Ed: Woehl. . . . Peters(1938)
         Concert.   Ed: Havemann. . . . . . . . . . . . . . B-N
         Trio Sonata--e mi, Hortus Musicus #25. . . . . . McG & M
VINEE   Trio-Serenade--F.   Fl, EH, Hp(Pf). . . . . . . . . . Gay & Teuton(1890)
WECKERLIN   Pastorale. . . . . . . . . . . . . . . . . . . . B-N
WEISSE   Concerto.   Fl, Ob, Hpschd. . . . . . . . . . . . . . .

---

*See remarks in Preface on instrumentation of Baroque Trio-Sonata editions.

## Fl, Cl, Pf(Hp)

BACH, J. S.   Adagio.   Arr: Fl, Ob(Vl, Cl), Pf by Sarlit.  . . . .  MBaron
BIZET   3 Pcs. from Bizet.   Arr.  . . . . . . . . . . .  Andraud
BRUNO   Recreation.  . . . . . . . . . . . . . . . . . . . . . . .
CLINTON   Grand Duo, Op 43.  . . . . . . . . . . . . . .  Ashdown
EMMANUEL   Trio Sonata. . . . . . . . . . . . . .  Lemoine(1907); MBaron
HAMM   Dialogue.   Fl, Ob(Cl), Pf. . . . . . . . . . . .  CFisch, B-N
IBERT   Aria.  . . . . . . . . . . . . . . . . . . .  MBaron
INGENHOVEN   Trio (1914-15).   Uses Hp.  . . . . . . . .  Senart(1920)
JOHNSON, HUNTER   Serenade (1937).  . . . . . . . . . .  Valley
LANGENUS   Scherzo-Swallow's Flight. . . . . . . . . . .
LECHTHALER   Freundliche Abendmusik.   Fl(Vl), Cl(Fl), Pf.  . .  Böhm(1942)
MIGOT   Divertissement Francaise.   Prelude, Estampie: Fl, Hp
                                   Prelude, Estampie: Cl, Hp
              Conclusion, double  Estampie: Fl, Cl, Hp. Leduc(1928); Andraud
OBIOLS   Divertimento. . . . . . . . . . . . . . .  Union mus. espan. (bef. 1900)
SAINT-SAENS   Tarantelle for Fl, Cl, Orch, Op 6(1857).   Arr.  . .  Durand; E-V
SCHMITT   Sonatine & Trio--E, Op 85.  . . . . . . . . .  Durand(1936); E-V
SWAN   Trio.  . . . . . . . . . . . . . . . . . . .  Belaiev(1936)
WALCKIERS   Trio--g mi, Op 95. . . . . . . . . . . . .  Costallat(c1860)
WILCOCKE   Trio.  . . . . . . . . . . . . . . . .  Rudall & Carte(c1910)

## Fl, Bn, Pf(Hp)

BEETHOVEN   Sonata--G, Op "259"(1786-90).   Fl(Vl), Bn(Vc), Pf.  B&H(1888); AMP
DUKELSKY   Trio-Var.  . . . . . . . . . . . . . . .  Edit. Russe(c1930)
HAYDN   Trios for Fl(Cl), Bn(Vc), Pf.   See Fl, Vc, Pf
HILL, ALF.   Miniature Trio #2--C.   Fl(Ob, Cl), Vc(Bn), Pf. . . .  GSch(1928)
JOLIVET   Pastorale de Noel.   Uses Hp. . . . . . . . . .  Merc
KOECHLIN   3 Pcs. , Op 34.  . . . . . . . . . . . . . . . .
LACOMBE, PAUL   Dialogue sentimental.   Vl(Fl), Bn(Vc), Pf. . .  Heugel(1917)
LEDUC   Trio, Op 66.   Fl, Vc(Bn), Pf.  . . . . . . . . . .  Leduc

## Fl, Hn, Pf

AUSTIN   In Field and Forest, Op 15.   Fl(Vl), Hn(Vc), Pf.  . . . .  Larway(1908)
HOLBROOKE   Trio--D, Op 28 [36?].   Fl(Vl), Hn, Pf.  . . . . .  Mod. Mus. Libr. (London, 1933)
MEL-BONIS   Suite, 4 mvts.  . . . . . . . . . . . . . . . . . . . .

## Ob, Cl, Pf

DESTENAY   Trio--b mi, Op 27.   . . . . . . . . . . . .  Hamelle(1906)
GABRIEL-MARIE   Feuilles au vent, 3 pcs.  . . . . . . . . .  MBaron
GILSON   Trio--g mi. . . . . . . . . . . . . . . . .  Cranz(1924)
KOPSCH   Trio--a mi. . . . . . . . . . . . . . . . .  UE(1929)

## Ob(EH), Bn, Pf

AGNEL   Pastoral--C, Op 1.   EH(Va), Bn(Vc), Pf.  . . . . . . .  Costallat(1864)
        Trio--D, Op 2.   Ob(Vl), Vc(Bn), Pf.  . . . . . . . .  Costallat; B-N

## Ob(EH), Bn, Pf cont.

BACH, W. FR.   Siziliano.   Ed: Weston.  . . . . . . . ... . . .   B&H(London, 1911)
BLANC   Trio--C, Op 14. . . . . . . . . . . . . . .   Costallat
BROD   Trio #1, Op 1.   . . . . . . . . . . . .   Costallat(new ed., 1877)
    Trio #2, Theme autriche, Op 11.   . . . . . . . .   Lemoine
    Trio #5, Op 24. . . . . . . . . . . . .   Lemoine
    Trio #7, Op 56. . . . . . . . . . . . .   Lemoine
CORTICELLI   Terzetto.   . . . . . . . . . . . . . . . .   Ricordi(c1840)
GRANDVAL   Grand Trio. . . . . . . . . . . . . . .   Lemoine(c1870)
    Trio de Salon.   . . . . . . . . . . . . . . . . . . .
HANDEL   Chamber Sonata #9--c mi, Op 1#8.   Ed: Seiffert. . . .   B&H(1915)
LALBER   Trio, Op 22. . . . . . . . . . . . . .   Peters(1872)
LALLIET   Terzetto--D, Op 22. . . . . . . . . . . . .   Hamelle(1872)
MOZART   2 Divertimenti for Winds--Eb, Bb; K ?.   Arr: Naumann.   B&H(1885)
PLANEL   Andante et Scherzo. . . . . . . . . . . . . .   MBaron
POULENC   Trio (1924-25).   . . . . . . . . . . . . .   Hansen(1926); McG & M

## Ob, Hn, Pf

HENRICH   Trio suite, Op 23.   . . . . . . . . . . .   Heinrichshofen(1937)
HERZOGENBERG   Trio--D, Op 61.   Ob(Vl), Hn(Va, Vc), Pf. . . .   Peters(1889)
KAHN   Serenade--f mi, Op 73.   Ob(Cl), Hn(Va, Vc), Pf. . . . .   Simrock(1923); AMP
REINECKE   Trio--a mi, Op 188. . . . . . . . . . . . . .   B&H(1887); AMP

## Cl, Bn, Pf

BEETHOVEN   3 Duos for Cl, Bn--C, F, Bb; Op"147." Pf acc. by Göhler . .   B&H(1900)
CIMR   Trio, Op 9.   Cl(Vl), Bn(Vc), Pf.   . . . . . . . . .   Urbanek(1905)
GLINKA   Pathetique--d mi (1827).   Cl(Vl), Bn(Vc), Pf. . . . .   Jurgenson(1889); Leeds
GOEPFART   Trio--g mi, Op 75. . . . . . . . . . . . .   F. Schuberth(1898)
GRIMM, FR. K.   Trio Sonata--Bb, Op 64. . . . . . . . . .   Mörike(1939)
HILL, ALF.   Miniature Trio #2--C.   Fl(Ob, Cl), Vc(Bn), Pf. . .   GSch(1928)
HOLBROOKE   Tamerlane. . . . . . . . . . . . . . .   Mod. Mus. Libr.
KREUTZER, KONR.   Trio--Eb, Op 43.   Bn or Vc. . . . . . .   Peters
LLOYD   Trio--Bb. . . . . . .. . . . . . . . .   Hawkes(c1900)
MOLBE   Songe--d mi, Op 80. . . . . . . . . . . . .   F. Rorich
NIKOLSKY   Elegie, Op 40#4. . . . . . . . . . . . . . .
POTTER   3 Trios, Op 12.   Vl(Cl), Vc(Bn), Pf. . . . . . .   Simrock
POULENC   Trio (1924-25).   See same under Ob, Bn, Pf. . . . .   MBaron
SCHNEIDER, FRIEDR.   Trio--Bb, Op 10.   . . . . . . . . .

## Cl, Hn, Pf(Hp)

ALEXANDER FRIEDRICH   Trio--A, Op 3. . . . . . . . .   Simrock(1897); AMP
HEIDRICH   Trio--c mi, Op 25. . . . . . . . . . . .   Kistner(1894); Andraud
KAHN   Serenade--f mi, Op 73.   Ob(Cl), Hn(Va, Vc), Pf. . . . .   Simrock(1923); AMP
REINECKE   Trio--Bb, Op 274.   . . . . . . . . . . .   B&H(1906); AMP
STRUBE   Trio (1936).   . . . . . . . . . . . . . . .
TOVEY   Style Tragique--c mi, Op 8.   Cl(Vl), Hn(Vc), Pf. . . . .   Schott(1906)
VOLKMANN   Schlummerlied, Op 76.   Uses Hp. . . . . . . .   Schott(1882)

## 2 Misc. Mixed Winds, Pf(Hpschd, Organ)

FICHER   Sonatina (1932).  Tt, Sx, Pf. . . . . . . . . . . . .   NME XII#1(1938)
GEBHARD, (LUDW.?)  Sonatine, Op 3.   Tt, Hn, Pf. . . . . . .   Böhm(1935)
MENDELSSOHN, F.   2 Concertstücke--f mi, d mi; Op113, 114.
                          Cl, BassetHn(AltCl), Pf.  . . . . . .   B&H; AMP
ROESGEN-CHAMPION   Concerto.   Sx, Bn, Hpschd. . . . . . . . . . . . . . .
RÜDINGER   Divertimento--g mi, Op 75.   Va(Cl), TenSx(BsCl, Vc), Pf. .   Böhm(1930)
WEBER, LUDW.   Festliches Stück.   Tt, Tb, Organ. . . . . . . . . . . .

## 3 INSTS.: 3 Similar Woodwinds

## 3 Fl

_____     3 & 4 Pt. Canons & Rounds.  3 or 4 Fl(Ob, Cl, Sx).  . .   Merc
ALBISI   Miniature Suite #1. . . . . . . . . . . . . . . .   C-B, B-N
         Miniature Suite #2.  Arr? . . . . . . . . . . . .   C-B
ANDRE   Trio--G, Op 29. . . . . . . . . . . . . . . .   Andre(1883); B-N
BACH, J.S.   Fughetta.  Arr: Taylor. . . . . . . . . .   Mills
BARRERE   2 Short Pcs. . . . . . . . . . . . . . . . .   CFisch
BEETHOVEN   Serenade--D, Op 25 (c1797).  Arr: Fetherston. . .   Belwin
            Trio for 2Ob, EH--C, Op 87.  Arr: Andraud. . . .   Andraud; MBaron
BERBIGUIER   Wrote 32 Trios for 3 Fl.
             2 Sets of Trios; Op 13, 110. . . . . . . . .   Ashdown
             Trio, Op 40. . . . . . . . . . . . . . . .   B&H
             Trio, Op 51. . . . . . . . . . . . . . . .   Schlesinger
CIARDI     Trio scolastico, Op 24. . . . . . . . . .   Ricordi(1853)
CLINTON   Trios--A, G, F; Op 7, 9, 30. . . . . . . . .   Ashdown
DRESSLER   Trio Concertante--D, Op 64. . . . . . . . .   Simrock
FAHRBACH   Trio, Op 58. . . . . . . . . . . . . . .   Ricordi(1865)
FÜRSTENAU   Trios--D, F, G; Op 14. . . . . . . . . . .   B&H
            Trio avec des Fugues--a mi, G, E; Op 22. . . . . .   Hansen
            Trio--F, Op 118. . . . . . . . . . . . .   Bote & Bock(1841)
GABRIELSKY   Numerous trios unpubl.
             Grand Trio Concert, Op 31. . . . . . . . .   Andraud
HAYDN   Rondo Scherzando.  Arr. . . . . . . . . . . .   Boosey
        Allegro Giocoso.  Arr: Taylor. . . . . . . . .   Mills
KOECHLIN   3 Divertissements, Op 91.  2Fl, BsFl(Cl). . . . . .   Andraud
KROLLMANN   Trios--D, F, e mi; Op 13. . . . . . . . . . . . .   . . .
KÜFFNER   Trio--D, Op 34. . . . . . . . . . . . . . .
KUHLAU   3 Trios--D, g mi, F; Op 13. . . . . . . . . . .   Costallat; MBaron
         3 Trios--e mi, D, Eb; Op 86. . . . . . . . . .   Cranz; B-N
         Trio--b mi, Op 90. . . . . . . . . . . . . .   Schott; B-N
KUMMER   Trios--G, D, C; Op 24, 30, 53. . . . . . . . .   Andre;
         Op24,     53.   Also arr: 3Cl.   . .   C-B
         Op    30, 53. . . . . . . . . . . .   B-N
         Trio #6--A, Op 59. . . . . . . . . . . . . .   Zimmerman; B-N
         2 Trios--d mi, G; Op 65, 72. . . . . . . . . .   B&H
LORENZO   Capriccio brillante, Op 31. . . . . . . . . .   Zimmerman(1930); B-N
MARTINENGHI   Terzetto. . . . . . . . . . . . . . . .   Ricordi
MATTHESON   Sonaten; Op 1#3-5, 8-10. . . . . . . . .   Nagel(1932-35)
MERCADANTE   3 Serenades. . . . . . . . . . . . . . .   Ricordi(1859); Belwin
MOZART   March from Titus [Clemenza di Tito, K 621. ?].  Arr: Taylor . .   Mills

**3 Fl** cont.

| | |
|---|---|
| NEUMANN   Trio--A, Op 14. . . . . . . . . . . . | Andre(1883); B-N |
| PAGANI   Trio, Op 7b. . . . . . . . . . . . . | Ricordi |
| QUANTZ   Sonate--D. Ed: Doflein. . . . . . . . | Nagel(1935); B-N |
| REICHA   Trio--D, Op 26. . . . . . . . . . . . . | . . . |
| SCHMID   Serenade, Op 99.   AltFl, TenFl, BsFl. . . . . . | Hieber(1935) |
| TULOU   Trio--Eb, Op 24. . . . . . . . . . . | Simrock |
|    Trio, Les trois amis--F, Op 65. . . . . . . . . | Cocks |
| WALCKIERS   Trio--F, Op 2. . . . . . . . . . | Zimmerman(1923); B-N |
|    2 Trios--D, Bb; Op 29, 37. . . . . . . . . | Joubert |
|    3 Trios--Eb, A, C; Op 93. . . . . . . . . | Richault |

**3 Ob(EH).**   (**2 Ob, EH** unless otherwise given. )

| | |
|---|---|
| ARDEVOL   4th Sonata a tres. . . . . . . . . . . . . . | Edit. Coop. ; SMPC |
| BACH, J. S.   Three Pt. Inventions.   Arr: Tustin. . . . . . . | Spratt |
| BEETHOVEN   Var. on Mozart's "La ci darem la mano"--C (c1797). | |
|    Ed: Stein. . . . . . . . . . . . | B&H(1914) |
|    Trio--C, Op 87 (1794?). . . . . . | B&H(1864), Costallat; AMP, Boosey |
| CADOW   Kleine Suite.   Ob(Fl), Ob, EH. . . . . . . . | Grosch(1942) |
| MAGANINI   Troubadours.   2Ob, Ob(EH). . . . . . . . | MBaron |
| MOSER, F. J.   Trio--c, Op 38. . . . . . . . . . | Bosworth(1926) |
| VOGT   Adagio religioso. . . . . . . . . . . . . | Costallat |

**3 Cl**

| | |
|---|---|
| _____   3 & 4 Pt. Canons & Rounds.   3 or 4 Fl(Ob, Cl, Sx). . . . | Merc |
| BACH, J. S.   Bach for the Clarinet.   Arr. , see same for 4 CL. . | GSch |
|    Sinfonia--c mi.   Arr: Cafarella. . . . . . . . | Witmark; MPHC |
| BEETHOVEN   1st mvt. of Trio 2Ob, EH--C, Op 87. Arr: Hernried. | Remick; MPHC |
| BLATT, (F. T. ?).   Trio, Op 27. . . . . . . . . . . . | Boosey |
| BLATT   Trio--Eb.   Ed: Bellison. . . . . . . . . . | Ricordi |
| BOUFFIL   Trios, Op 7#1, 2, 3. . . . . . . . . . | C-B |
|    Trios--G, a mi, F; Op 8. . . . . . . . . | Schott(1886) |
| BOVE   Andante & Allegro.   2Cl, BsCl(Bn). . . . . . . . | Leeds |
| CARULLI   Trio--Bb.   Ed: Bellison. . . . . . . . . | Ricordi |
| CHANDLER   Eudora. . . . . . . . . . . . . . | Pro-Art |
| COHEN   Madrigale.   2Cl, BsCl. . . . . . . . . . | Belwin |
| HANDEL   Sonata--D.   Arr. . . . . . . . . . . | Merc |
| HAUBIEL   In the Phrygian Mode. . . . . . . . . . | CompPr |
| HÖFFER   Die Herzenhoch.   3Cl or other combinations. . . . . | Vieweg(1938) |
| KUMMER   Fl Trios--G, C. A; Op 24, 53, 59.   Arr: 3Cl. . . . . | C-B |
| MIHALOVICI   Sonate, Op 35.   Eb Cl, A Cl, BsCl. . . . . . | Salabert(1933); MBaron |
| MORITZ, EDV.   Divertimento.   Cl, 2Cl(Sx). . . . . . . . | Merc |
| MÜLLER, IWAN   Trio--g mi.   Ed: Bellison. . . . . . . . | Ricordi |
| PLEYEL   6 Duets, Op 8.   Arr: 3Cl. . . . . . . . . | C-B |
| STARK   Sonata--g mi.   2Cl, BassetHn(AltCl, Bn). . . . . . | Schmidt (1897) |
| TUTHILL   Intermezzo, Op 1#2 (1927).   2Cl, BassetHn(AltCl) . . | CFisch |
| VOGT   Adagio Religioso for 2Ob, EH.   Arr: 3Cl by Voxman. . . | Rubank |
| WATERSON   Trio Concertante--g mi. . . . . . . . . . | Boosey, C-B |
| ZÖLLER   Sonate, Op 158. . . . . . . . . . . . . | Boosey(1885) |

## 3 Bn

BANTOCK    Dance of Witches, Rondo. . . . . . . . . . . Swan(London, 1927)
BERGT    Trio, 4 mvts. . . . . . . . . . . . . . . Hofmeister(1880, 1933)
FUCHS, (G. F. ?)    Six Trios, Op 1. . . . . . . . . . . . Lemoine
WEISSENBORN    6 Pieces, Op 4. . . . . . . . . . . . Hofmeister(1933)


## 3 INSTS.: 3 Mixed Woodwinds

### 2 Fl, Cl

_____Collection, 18 Trios from Classic* Masters. Fl(Vl), Ob(Fl, Vl), Cl.
                Ed: Leeuwen, Andraud. . . . . . . . . . . . . . Andraud
DAQUIN    La Joyeuse.  Fl, Fl(Ob), Cl. . . . . . . . . . . . . Andraud
KOECHLIN    3 Divertissements, Op 91.  2Fl, BsFl(Cl). . . . . . . . . . Andraud
MARTINI    Les Moutons.  Fl, Fl(Ob), Cl.  Arr: Milhaud. . . . . . . Andraud


### Fl, Ob, Cl

_____Collection, 18 Trios from Classic* Masters.  Fl(Vl), Ob(Fl, Vl), Cl.
                Ed: Leeuwen, Andraud. . . . . . . . . . . . . Andraud
BOCCHERINI    Terzetto.  Fl, Ob(Cl), Cl.  Arr: Waln. . . . . . . . Kjos
CARION    Bagatelles. . . . . . . . . . . . . . . . . . MBaron
DAHLHOFF    Burlesque, Allegretto, Scherzo. . . . . . . . Schmidt(1925); Andraud
DAQUIN    La Joyeuse.  Fl, Fl(Ob), Cl. . . . . . . . . . Andraud
GENARRO    Trio--G. . . . . . . . . . . . . . Evette & S.(1922); Andraud
JEMNITZ    Trio, Op 20. . . . . . . . . . . . . . Zimmerman(1928)
KRIENS    Ronde des Lutins. . . . . . . . . . . . . . Andraud
KUHLAU    Sonatina, Op 20#1.  Arr: Tustin. . . . . . . . . Spratt
MARTINI    Les Moutons.  Fl, Fl(Ob), Cl.  Arr: Milhaud. . . . Andraud
MOSER, RUD.    Divertimento, Op 51#1. . . . . . . . . Steingräber(1933); Andraud
OLIVADOTI    Scherzetto.  Fl, Ob(Cl), Cl. . . . . . . . . Remick; MPHC
OLSEN    Suite. . . . . . . . . . . . . . . . . Peters; MBaron
SCHMID    Serenade, Op 99. . . . . . . . . . . . . .
VILLA-LOBOS    Trio (1921). . . . . . . . . . . . . . .
WAILLY    Aubade. . . . . . . . . . . . . . . . . Rubank, B-N
WIENER    3 Pcs., Op 20.  Duo:        Fl, EH
                Intermezzo: Fl, Cl
                Terzett:    Fl, EH, Cl . . . . . . . UE(1931); Andraud


### Fl, 2 Cl

ALBISI    Miniature Suite #2  . . . . . . . . . . . . . . . C-B
ARTOT, J. B.    12 Trios.  Fl(Cl), Cl, Cl(AltSx). . . . . . . . C-B
BOCCHERINI    Terzetto.  Fl, Ob(Cl), Cl.  Arr: Waln. . . . . Kjos
COBB    Woodland Dance. . . . . . . . . . . . . . . Remick; MPHC
KUBIK    Little Suite. . . . . . . . . . . . . . . . Hargail
OLIVADOTI    Scherzetto.  Fl, Ob(Cl), Cl.  . . . . . . . . . Remick; MPHC


*Actually includes Pre- and Post- Classical Masters.

## Fl, Ob, Bn

| | | |
|---|---|---|
| BULLING | Suite, Op 30. . . . . . . . . . . . . . . . . | Grosch(1942) |
| FORTNER | Serenade (1945). . . . . . . . . . . . . . . | Schott; AMP, MBaron |
| MAGANINI | Vienna.   Fl, Ob(Cl), Bn. . . . . . . . . . . . | CFisch |
| NEWMAN | Rondo Brillante.   Arr: Taylor. . . . . . . . | Mills |
| RÖNTGEN | Trio--G, Op 86. . . . . . . . . . . . | Alsbach(1931) |
| TELEMANN | Trio--c mi.   Arr: Fl, Ob(Cl), Bn. . . . . . . . | Andraud |

## Fl, Cl, Bn

| | | |
|---|---|---|
| _____ | 3 Little Classics.   Fl(Ob), Cl, Bn.   Ed: Hirsch.   . . . | Witmark; MPHC |
| BACH, J. S. | Fugue from W. T. C. --c mi.   Arr: Tarlow. . . . . | E-V |
| | Sinfonia IX, XI, & Gavotte.   Arr: T. Finney. . . . | Witmark; MPHC |
| BECKERATH | Musik--D.   Vl(Fl, Ob), Cl, Vc(Bn). | Litolff(1938) |
| BEETHOVEN | Var. on Mozart's "La ci darem la mano" for | |
| |           2Ob, EH--C.   Arr: Weigelt. . . . . . | Leuckart(1932) |
| | Trio for 2Ob, EH--C, Op 87.   Arr: Weigelt. . . | Leuckart |
| | ditto . . . . . . . . . . . . . . . | MBaron |
| BENTZON | Sonatine, Op 7.   . . . . . . . . . . . | Borups Musikförlag(1926); McG & M |
| BOVE | Petit Trio.   Fl(Ob), Cl, Bn. . . . . . . . . . | CFisch(1934) |
| CAMARA | Suite. . . . . . . . . . . . . . . . . | Edit. Coop. ; SMPC |
| CARMAN, A. | Petit Rondo.   Fl(Cl), Cl, Bn. . . . . . . . . | C-B |
| FRANCO, (J. H. G. ?) | Sonata a tre. . . . . . . . . . . . . | Ricordi(1935) |
| JOSTEN | Trio (1940). . . . . . . . . . . . . . . . | Arrow |
| KOECHLIN | Trio--G, Op 92. . . . . . . . . . . . . . | Senart(1928) |
| KOTSCHAU | Divertimento--Bb, Op 12a. . . . . . . . . . . | Zimmerman(1932); Rubank |
| KUHLAU | Allegro, Op 20#2.   Arr: Fl, Cl, Bn(BsCl) by Tustin. . | Spratt |
| KUMMER | Trio--F, Op 32.   Fl, Cl(Vl), Bn(Vc). . . . . . . | Andre(1864); Andraud |
| LORENZO | 2 Divertimenti; Op 24, 29.   . . . . . . . . | Zimmerman(1931); Andraud |
| MAGANINI | Ars Contrapunctus. . . . . . . . . . . . | MBaron |
| | Havana & Istamboul.   Fl(Ob), Cl, Bn. . . . . . . | CFisch |
| | Vienna.   Fl(Ob), Cl, Bn. . . . . . . . . . . | CFisch |
| MONDONVILLE | Tambourin.   Fl(Ob), Cl, Bn. . . . . . . . . | Andraud |
| MOZART | #1, 4 from 5 Divertimenti for 2Cl, Bn--all Bb, K Anh 229. | |
| |         Arr: Weigelt. . . . . . . . . . . . | Leuckart(1932) |
| PARADISI | Sonata.   Arr: Horton. . . . . . . . . . . . | Remick; MPHC |
| PERCEVAL | Serenata. . . . . . . . . . . . . . . . . . | Edit. Coop. ; SMPC |
| PIJPER | Trio.   . . . . . . . . . . . . . . . . . . . . . . | |
| PISTON | 3 Pcs. (1926). . . . . . . . . . . . . . | NME VI#4(1933); Andraud |
| RORICH | Trio in Contrapontal Style--C, Op 81b. . . . . . . | Zimmerman(1930); Andraud |
| SHOSTAKOVITCH | Preludes [for Pf?].   Arr: Fl(Ob), Cl, Bn. . . | Edit. Musicus; MBaron |
| SPRATT | 3 Miniatures. . . . . . . . . . . . . . . | MBaron |
| STRINGFIELD | Chipmunks. . . . . . . . . . . . . . . . | Edit. Musicus; MBaron |
| TELEMANN | Trio--c mi.   Arr: Fl, Ob(Cl), Bn. . . . . . . . | Andraud |
| WALCKIERS | 3 Trios--Bb, F, c mi; Op 12. . . . . . . . . | Richault |
| WEIS | Trio.   . . . . . . . . . . . . . . . . . | Kistner(1930);McG & M |
| WEISS | Trio (1937). . . . . . . . . . . . . | Boletin Latino Americano |
| ZOELLER, (K?). | 3 Virtuosos, Musical Joke. . . . . . . . . | Boosey |

## 2 Ob(EH), 1 Misc.

BACH, J. S.    Fughetta.  Arr: Ob, EH, Bn by Cafarella.   . . . .  Witmark: MPHC
BONNEAU    3 Ancient Noels.  Ob, EH(Cl), Bn. . . . . . . . .  Andraud
KARG-ELERT   Trio--d mi, Op 49#1.  Ob, EH(Hn), Cl.  . . . .  Hofmeister(1905); Andraud
MARAIS    Petite Trio d'Alcyone.   2Ob, Bn.   . . . . . . . .  Andraud

## Ob, Cl, Bn

_____    3 Little Classics.  Arr: Fl(Ob), Cl, Bn by Hirsch.   . . .  Witmark; MPHC
AURIC    Trio (1938). . . . . . . . . . . . . . . . .  Andraud
BACH, J. S.   Gavotte & Musette.  Arr: Leeuwen. . . . . . . . .  Remick; MPHC
              Prelude & Fugue.  Arr: Oubradous.   . . . . . .  Lyrebird; MBaron
              Prelude  & Fugue.  Arr: Arnell. . . . . . . . .  Boosey
BACH, (J. S. ?)   Polonaise--g mi.  Arr. . . . . . . . . . .  Presser
BACH, J. S.    Sinfonia IX, XI, & Gavotte.   Arr: Fl(Ob), Cl, Bn
              by Finney.   . . . . . . . . . . . . . . .  Witmark; MPHC
BANES    Shepherds Pipe, Villanelle. . . . . . . . . . . .  Societe Nouvelle; Andraud
BARRAUD   Trio.    . . . . . . . . . . . . . . . . .  Lyrebird(1939); MBaron
BECKERATH   Musik--D.   Vl(Fl, Ob), Cl, Vc(Bn). . . . . . .  Litolff(1938)
BECLARD d'HARCOURT    Rapsodie peruvienne.   . . . . . . .  Lemoine; E-V
BENTZON    Racconto #3. . . . . . . . . . . . . . . .  McG & M
BONNEAU    3 Ancient Noels.  Ob, EH(Cl), Bn. . . . . . . .  Andraud
BOVE   Petit Trio.   Fl(Ob), Cl, Bn. . . . . . . . . . .  CFisch(1934)
BOZZA    Suite Breve.    . . . . . . . . . . . . . .  Andraud, MBaron
DAVID, HANS    Introduction & Fugue in 18th-C. Style. . . . .  Ms available U. of Mich.
DECRUCK    Capriccio. . . . . . . . . . . . . . . . .  Andraud
              Le P'tite Quinquin. . . . . . . . . . . .  Andraud
FERROUD    Trio--E.   . . . . . . . . . . . . . . . .  Durand(1934); E-V
FLEGIER    Suite--B.  . . . . . . . . . . . . . . . .  Gallet(1897); Andraud
GALLON    Suite. . . . . . . . . . . . . . . . . . .  Andraud, MBaron
GOLESTAN    Divertimento. . . . . . . . . . . . . . .  . . . . .
GOUE    Bagatell, Melopee, Scherzo. . . . . . . . . . .  Andraud
HAHN    Eglogue.   . . . . . . . . . . . . . . . . .  Andraud
HUGUENIN    Trios:  Op 30, 31. . . . . . . . . . . . .  Andraud
IBERT    Pcs.  & Trio. . . . . . . . . . . . . . . .  Andraud
IKONOMOV    Trio--E, Op 14. . . . . . . . . . . . . .  Lyrebird(1937); MBaron
IPPOLITOV-IVANOV    Zwei Kirgische Lieder. . . . . . . . .  Merc, McG & M
JEAN-MARTINON   Sonatine #4.  . . . . . . . . . . . .  MBaron
JONGEN    Trio. . . . . . . . . . . . . . . . . . .  Andraud
JUON    Arabesken, Op 73. . . . . . . . . . . . . . .  Schott(1941)
KREJCI    Trio.   . . . . . . . . . . . . . . . . .  . . . . .
MAGANINI    La Rubia. . . . . . . . . . . . . . . . .  Andraud
              Havana; Istamboul; Vienna. . . . . . . . .  CFisch
MARTELLI    Trio.   . . . . . . . . . . . . . . . .  Andraud
MELKIKH    Trio--f# mi, Op 17. . . . . . . . . . . . .  UE(1928); Peters
MIGOT    Threnody.   . . . . . . . . . . . . . . . .  Leduc; MBaron
MILHAUD    Suite d'apres Corette. . . . . . . . . . . .  Lyrebird; Broude
              Pastorale. . . . . . . . . . . . . . . .  Senart(1937); E-V
MONDONVILLE    Tambourin.  Arr: Fl(Ob), Cl, Bn. . . . . . .  Andraud
MOZART    5 Divertimenti for 2Cl, Bn--all Bb, K Anh 229.  Arr..  Andraud
              4th Divertimento [from above?]. . . . . . . .  Broude
ORBAN    Prelude, Pastorale, Divertimento.  . . . . . . .  Andraud
OUBRADOUS    Sonatine.  . . . . . . . . . . . . . . .  MBaron
PFEIFFER, (G. ?)   Musette, Op 47.  . . . . . . . . . .  Andraud
PIERNE, PAUL    Bucolique Variee. . . . . . . . . . . .  Andraud

## Ob, Cl, Bn cont.

| | | |
|---|---|---|
| RIVIER, (JEAN?) | Petite Suite. | Andraud |
| ROUSSEL | Andante from unfinished Trio. | Andraud |
| SCHMIT | Trio. | MBaron |
| SCHULHOFF | Divertissement. | Schott(1928); AMP |
| SHOSTAKOVITCH | Preludes [for Pf?]. Fl(Ob), Cl, Bn. | Edit. Musicus; MBaron |
| SZALOWSKI | Trio. | MBaron |
| TOMASI | Concert Champetre. | MBaron |
| VILLA-LOBOS | Trio. | Eschig(1929); AMP, IMC |
| VAUBOURGOIN | Trio. | MBaron |
| WAGNER-REGENY | Suite. | UE(1929) |
| WALTHEW | Triolet--Eb. | Boosey(1934) |
| WISSMER | Serenade. | Andraud |

## 2 Cl, Bn

| | | |
|---|---|---|
| BACH, J. S. | 3 Fugues. Arr. | Boosey |
| BOVE | Andante & Allegro. 2Cl, BsCl(Bn). | Leeds |
| CARMAN, A. | Petit Rondo. Cl(Fl), Cl, Bn. | C-B |
| FUCIK | Fantasy on Bohemian Folksong. | Edit. Continental(Prague, 1939) |
| HENNESSY | Trio--G, Op 54. | Eschig(1921); AMP, MBaron |
| JELINEK | 6 kleine Stücke. | UE(1922); Peters |
| LANGE, G. FR. | Die drei lustigen Bruder. | Erdmann(1881) |
| MOZART | Kanonisches Adagio--F, K 410. 2BassetHn(AltCl),Bn. | B&H(1885) |
| | 5 Divertimenti--all Bb, K Anh 229. Ed: Lewicki. | B&H |
| | ditto | Ed: T. Finney. | Witmark; MPHC |
| | #1, 2 of above. | Boosey |
| SOBECK | Trio--F, Op 20. Bn or Vc. | Erler(1898) |
| STARK | Sonata--g mi. 2Cl, BassetHn(Bn). | Schmidt(1897) |
| WALTHEW | Prelude & Fugue. 2Cl, Bn(Vc). | |
| ZOELLER, (K?). | Auf der Alm. | Boosey |

## 3 INSTS. : 3 Brass

## 3 Hn

| | | |
|---|---|---|
| BEETHOVEN | Trio for 2Ob, EH--C, Op 87. Arr: Gumbert. | Kistner(1882) |
| DAUPRAT | 3 Grand Trios, Op 4. | Lemoine(c1815) |
| | Grand Trio, Op 26. | Lemoine(c1840) |
| | 6 Trios & 6 Quartets, Op 8. | Lemoine(c1840) |
| FREHSE | 12 Trios, Op 10. | Hofmeister(1929); Sansone |
| KLING | 30 selected pcs. Arr: Teague. | Broadcast; AMP |
| REICHA | 6 of 12 Trios, Op 82. Ed: Gumbert. | Hofmeister(1882) |
| SCHNEIDER, G. A. | 18 Trios, Op 56. | B&H |
| STICH | 20 Trios. | |

## 3 Misc. Brass

| | | |
|---|---|---|
| _____ | 5 Pre-Classical Pcs. 3Ct(Tt). Ed: Goldman. | Merc |
| ARDEVOL | 3rd Sonata a Tres. 2Tt, Tb. | Edit. Coop.; SMPC |
| BAMBERG | Trios, 2 Books. 3Tb. | Hofmeister |
| HANSEN, ARNO | 65 Trios. 3Tb. | Hofmeister |
| HAUBIEL, (CHAS. ?) | Acceleration. 3Tt. | Belwin |

3 Misc. Brass cont.

O'NEILL      Autumn Tones.    3Ct(Tt). . . . . . . . . . . . . Merc
PHILLIPS     Trio for Trumpets. (1937). . . . . . . . . . . . . . . . . . . . .
POULENC     Sonata--G (1922).    Tt, Hn, Tb. . . . . . . . . Chester(1924), Schott; MBaron
SCHIFFMANN     Fantasie.    3Tb. . . . . . . . . . . . . . Hofmeister(1941)
VIERDANCK     Capricci for 2 & 3 Tt.    (Orig. for Zinken). . . . McG & M

## 3 INSTS. :   3 Misc. Winds

_____     3 & 4 Pt.  Canons & Rounds.    3 or 4 Fl(Ob, Cl, Sx). . . . Merc
ARTOT, J. B.    12 Trios.    Fl(Cl), Cl, Cl(Sx). . . . . . . . . C-B
CADOW    Kleine Suite.    Ob(Fl), Ob, EH. . . . . . . . . . . Grosch(1942)
CRUSELL     Trio.    Cl, Hn, Bn. . . . . . . . . . . . . . . . . . . .
HANDEL     Sonata--d mi.    2Cl, Hn.    Ed: Coopersmith, LaRue. . Merc, McG & M
KARG-ELERT     Trio--d mi, Op 49#1.    Ob, Cl, EH(Hn). . . . . Hofmeister(1905); Andraud
MORITZ, EDV.    Divertimento.    Cl, Cl(Sx), Cl(Sx). . . . . . . Merc
PANNIER     Trio--Eb, Op 40.    Cl, Hn, Bn. . . . . . . . . . Grosch(1938); Andraud
WILLAERT    9 Ricercari in 3 Pts.    3 Winds(Sopr, Alto, Bs). . . . Schott; AMP

# FOUR INSTRUMENTS

## 4 INSTS. : including 1 Wind

Fl, Vl, Va, Vc unless otherwise given.

AMON    3 Quartets--C, D, G; Op 113#1-3. . . . . . . . . . . Andre(1878

BACH, J. C.    3 Quartets--C, Eb, G; Op 8#1, 3, 5.    Ed: Kuster,
              Gloder. . . . . . . . . . . . . Bärenreiter; McG & M

BENEDICT    Quartet, Op 21. . . . . . . . . . . . . . . Mills

BERBIGUIER    Quar--C, Op 86. . . . . . . . . . . . . . .

BORODIN    Quar [for Strs?].    Fl(Vl), Ob(Vl), Va, Vc. . . . Leeds

BOURGAULT-DUCOUDRAY    Quar. . . . . . . . . . . . . . Lemoine

CADOW    Var. on a Norwegian Folksong--g mi. . . . . . . . Grosch(1934)

CRUSELL    Quar--D, Op 8. . . . . . . . . . . . . . . Peters(1843)

DRESSLER    3 Quar--A, D, C; Op 10, 30, 37. . . . . . . . B&H

EICHNER    Quar--D, Op 4#4.    Ed: Riemann in D. T. B. XXVII. . B&H(1914)

FÜRSTENAU    4 Quar--E, Ab, F, g mi; Op 39, 60, 62, 74. . . . . Andre

GABRIELSKI    Quar--D, C; Op 60, 95. . . . . . . . . . . Probst

GYROWETZ    3rd Nocturne--G, Op 26.    Ed: Altmann. . . . . Zimmerman(1933); Andraud

HANSEL, P.    Quart, Op 17. . . . . . . . . . . . . . . Schott

HAYDN    Der Geburtstag.    Ed: Lemacher, Mies. . . . . . Tonger(1932)

HENNESSY    Var. on Theme of 6 Notes, Op 58. . . . . . . . Eschig(1925); AMP

HINDEMITH    Abendkonzert Quar., from "Plöner Musiktag"(1932) Schott; AMP

HOFFMEISTER    Quar. . . . . . . . . . . . . . . . Schott

HOYER    Elegie, 3 voice Canon.    2Fl(Vl), Va, Vc(Bn). . . . Portius(1937)

KRAFT    Kleine Hausmusik. . . . . . . . . . . . . . Robert(Lübeck, 1939)

KROMMER    2 Quar--F, C; Op 17, 30. . . . . . . . . . . . .

KUHN    Abendstimmung--D. . . . . . . . . . . . . . Ries & E. (1934)

KUMMER    2 Quar--C, d mi; Op 54, 102. . . . . . . . . Schott

           Quar--D, Op 89. . . . . . . . . . . . . Andre(1863)

           Quar--C, e mi, d mi, A; Op 37, 47, 49, 90. . . . . . .

           Quar--G, D, C; Op 99#1-3. . . . . . . . . . .

LEFEBVRE    Quar, Op 102. . . . . . . . . . . . . . Hamelle(c1900)

MARX    Little Suite after L. Mozart Notebook. . . . . . . . Hanseat(Hamburg, 1939)

MORALT    Quar. . . . . . . . . . . . . . . . . . Falter(Munich)

        Quar. . . . . . . . . . . . . . . . . Sidler(Munich)

MOZART    2 Quar--D, A; K 285(1777), K 298(1778). . . . . . B&H(1882); AMP

        ditto above, K 285.    Ed: Einstein. . . . . . . . . McG & M

        Quar--G, K 285a.    Ed: Einstein. . . . . . . . . Hinrichsen(1938); MBaron

        Quar--C, K 285b or K Anh 171 [K"631"]. . . . . . IMC, MBaron

PLEYEL    6 Quar. . . . . . . . . . . . . . . . . . Andre

PRÄGER, H. A.    Quar--D, Op 20. . . . . . . . . . . . B&H

REICHA    6 Quar--e mi, A, D, g mi, C, G; Op 98 . . . . . . . Schott

RIES    3 Quar--C, e mi, A; Op 145. . . . . . . . . . . Simrock

ROSSINI    Quar--G, A, Bb, D.    Arr. . . . . . . . . . Schott

SCHAFFNER    3 Quar, Op 7. . . . . . . . . . . . . . Costallat

           2 Quar, Op 29. . . . . . . . . . . . . . .

SCHNEIDER, G. A.    6 Quar--D, F, d mi, G, Bb, g mi; Op 51. . . . B&H

                3 Quar--D, F, G; Op 52. . . . . . . . . B&H

SCHWINDL    Quar--G, Op 7#1.    Ed: Lenzewski, Sr. . . . . . Vieweg(1926)

THIERIOT    Quar--G, Op 84. . . . . . . . . . . . . . Peters(1905)

TOESCHI    Quar--G, Op 1#4.    Ed: Riemann in D. T. B. XXVII. . . B&H(1914)

VIOTTI    3 Quar--Bb, c mi, Eb; Op 22. . . . . . . . . . . .

Fl, Vl, Va, Vc cont.

VOGLER    Quar--Bb.   Ed: Riemann in D. T. B. XXVII. . . . . .   B&H(1914)
WAILLY    Serenade--a mi, Op 25. . . . . . . . . . . . .   Rouart(c1900)
WALCKIERS    3 Quar, Op 5.   . . . ' . . . . . . . . .   Costallat(1820)
                Quar--D, Op 50. . . . . . . . . . . .   B&H
WENDLING    Quar--G, Op 10#6.   Ed: Riemann in D. T. B. XXVII.  B&H(1914)


Ob(EH), Vl, Va, Vc unless otherwise given.

BACH, J. C.    Quar--C, Eb, G; Op 8#1, 3, 5.   Fl(Ob, Cl), Vl, Va, Vc.
                Ed: Kuster, Gloder.  . . . . . . . . . .   Bärenreiter; McG & M
BEYTHIEN    Quar--Bb, Op 24. . . . . . . . . . . . . .   Author publ. (Dresden, 1937)
BRITTEN    Fantasia. . . . . . . . . . . . . . . . . .   Boosey(1935); Andraud
CADOW    Var. on a Norwegian Folksong--g mi.   Fl(Ob), Vl, Va, Vc.  Grosch(1934)
DONOVAN    Serenade. . . . . . . . . . . . . . . . .   NME XIV#3(1941)
HAUBIEL    Masque (1937). . . . . . . . . . . . . . . .
HAYDN    Divertimento--Bb.   Ob, Vl, Gamba(Va), Cb.   Ed: Dolmetsch . . .   OUP(1931)
HENNESSY    Four celtic pieces, Op 59.   For EH. . . . . . .   Eschig(1925); AMP
HÖFFER    Serenade--G, Op 43. . . . . . . . . . . . .   Litolff(1937); Andraud
MOZART    Quar--F, K 370 (1781). . . . . . . . . . .   B&H(1882); AMP, McG & M
PHILLIPS    Quar (1937). . . . . . . . . . . . . . . . .
RIPFEL    Quar. . . . . . . . . . . . . . . . . . . .   Schott
STAMITZ    Quar--Eb, Op 8#4.   Ob or Cl.   Ed: v. Dameck.  . . .   Raabe(1919); Andraud


Cl, Vl, Va, Vc

BACH, J. C.    Quar--C, Eb, G; Op 8#1, 3, 5.   Fl(Ob, Cl), Vl, Va, Vc.
                Ed: Kuster, Gloder. . . . . . . . . . .   Bärenreiter; McG & M
BÄRMANN    Quar--Bb, Op 18. . . . . . . . . . . . .   Schott(1882)
BOCHSA    Several Quartets.  . . . . . . . . . . . . . . .
CRUSELL    4 Quar--Eb, Bb, B, D; Op 2, 4, 7, 8. . . . . . . .   Peters(1840-42)
GÖPFERT    3 Quar; Op 2, 16. . . . . . . . . . . . . .   Andre
HINDEMITH    Abendkonzert Quar. , from "Plöner Musiktag"(1932)  Schott(1932); AMP
INGENHOVEN    5 Chamber Music Pcs. . . . . . . . . . .   Tischer & J. (1935); Andraud
KINZI    Quar--F. . . . . . . . . . . . . . . . . . .   Schott(1882)
KREUTZER, KONR.    Quar. . . . . . . . . . . . . . .
                Andante Grazioso [from above, 2nd mvt. ?]   Alfred
MÜLLER, FR.    Quar--Bb, Op 80. . . . . . . . . . .   Hofmeister(1860)
MÜLLER, S. W.    Chamber Music--A, Op 1. . . . . . . .   B&H(1928); AMP
PUGNI    3 Quar.  . . . . . . . . . . . . . . . . . .   Ricordi
RAWSTHORNE    Quar. . . . . . . . . . . . . . . .
SCHMIDT, F.    3 Quar.   Cl, Strs. . . . . . . . . . .   Leduc
STAMITZ    Quar--Eb, Op 8#4.   Ob(Cl), Vl, Va, Vc.   Ed: v. Dameck  . .   Raabe(1919); Andraud
                Quar--Eb, Op 8 #4. . . . . . . . . . . .   IMC, MBaron
                2 Quar.   Cl(Fl, Ob), Vl, Va, Vc. . . . . . . .   Merc, McG & M
TROWBRIDGE    Quar. . . . . . . . . . . . . . . . .   CompPr(1945)
WALTER, ALB.    6 Quar.   Cl, Strs. . . . . . . . . . .   Pleyel

## Misc. including 1 Wind

ALMENRAEDER   Var. on an Ancient Melody.   Bn, Vl, Va, Vc.   .  Spratt
MATIEGKA      Quar--G (1814).   Fl, Va, Vc, Guitar.  Arr: Fr. Schubert . . B&H
STICH  24 Quar.   Hn, StrTrio. . . . . . . . . . . . . . . . . . . .


## 4 INSTS.:   including 1 Wind & Pf(Keyboard, etc. )*

Fl, Vl, Vc, Pf unless otherwise given.

_____  Masters of the Baroque, Collection of Trio Sonatas.
          Ed. for 2Fl(Vl), Pf, Vc ad lib.   . . . . . .  Peters
_____  Collegium Musicum, Collection of nearly 60 17th-& 18th-
          Cent. chamber music works.   2Vl(Fl, Ob), Pf, Vc ad lib . .  B & H
BACH, J. C.   2 Sonatas. . . . . . . . . . . . . . . . . . . Andraud
BACH, J. S.   Trio Sonata--G. . . . . . . . . . . . . . . . MBaron
          Trio Sonata--c mi, from Musical Offering.
                    Ed: David . . . . . . . . . . . . GSch
          ditto . . . Ed: Rabaud . . . . . . . . . . B&H; AMP
          ditto . . . Ed: Landshoff . . . . . . . . . Peters(1937)
BACH, K. P. E.   3 Quar--G, a mi, D.   Fl, Va, Vc, Pf. Ed: Schmid . . Bisping; Andraud
          Trio Sonata--Bb.   Ed: Landshoff. . .`. . . . . Peters(1936); IMC
          Trio--b mi.   Ed: Ermeler. . . . . . . . . Zimmerman(1932)
BACH, W. FR.   Sonata. . . . . . . . . . . . . . . . Peters
          Sonata--Bb.   Ed: Seiffert. . . . . . . . . B&H(1931); IMC
BEETHOVEN   Septet--Eb, Op 20.   Arr: Hummel. . . . . . . . . . . . . . . . .
BERNARD, J.   Pastorale--d mi. . . . . . . . . . . . . Hayet(1921)
CASTERA   Concerto--A (1911-12).   Fl, Cl(Vl), Vc, Pf. . . . . Rouart(1924); Andraud
DOPPLER   Nocturne, Op 19.   Fl, Vl, Hn(Vc), Pf.  . . . . . Andraud
DUNHILL   Berceuse & Minuet.   Fl(Ob), Vl, Va, Pf. . . . . . Augener(1937)
DUPORQUIER   Pastorale. . . . . . . . . . . . . . . . Heugel(1892)
FRESCOBALDI   5 Canzoni a 2 canti.   2Fl(Vl), Pf, Vc(Bn) ad lib.
                    Ed: H. David. . . . . . . . . . . . Schott; AMP, MBaron
GRAUN   Trio Sonate--F.   Ed: Fischer, Wittenbecher. . . . . Zimmerman(1934)
GRETRY   2 Quar, Op 1. . . . . . . . . . . . . . . . Andre
GUILLEMAIN   Conversation Galante, Op 12#1.   Ed: Mengel. . B&H; AMP
HANDEL   See 4 INSTS.: including 2 Winds & Pf.
          Sonatas 1, 2--c mi, F.   Ed: Mönkemeyer. . . . . . Schott(1939)
HASLINGER   Quar--G.   Fl, Va, Vc, Pf. . . . . . . . . . Haslinger
KEISER   Trio Sonata #1, 2, 3--D, G, D.   Ed: Schenk. . . . Nagel(1931-37); AMP
KEMPFF   Quar--G, Op 15. . . . . . . . . . . . . . Simrock(1925)
KREBS   Suite with Overture--D.   Ed: Riemann, Coll. Mus#31. B&H(1906); AMP
LECLAIR   Trio--D, Op 2#8.   Fl(Vl), Va, Pf, Vc ad lib. . . . . Schott; AMP
          ditto . . . . . . F l(Vl), Gamba(Vc), Pf, Vc ad lib. Schott; AMP
LEGRENZI   Sonata--d mi (1655).   2Fl(Vl), Pf, Vc ad lib. . . . Peters
LOCATELLI   Trio--G, Op 3#1.   2Fl(Vl), Pf, Vc.   Ed: Riemann . B&H(1906); AMP
MIGOT   Quar.   Fl(Vl), Vl, Cl(Va), Hp. . . . . . . . . . SireneM(1927); Andraud
MOZART   German Dance--a mi.   Fl(Vl), Ob(Vl), Bn(Vc), Pf ad lib . . Peters
MYSLIWECEK   Trio--Bb, Op 1#4.   Ed: Riemann, Coll. Mus. #20 . . B&H(1904); AMP, IMC

_____

*See remarks in Preface on instrumentation of Baroque chamber music editions.  Several combi-
nations of instruments are possible and authentic.

Fl, Vl, Vc, Pf unless otherwise given; cont.

PAISABLE    Sonatas--d, g, F, c, C; Nr 1-5.   2Fl(Ob, Vl), Pf, Vc.
                        Ed: Friedrich . . . . . . . . . . . . .   Moeck(1939); McG & M
PEPUSCH   Trio Sonata--g mi.   Fl, Ob(Vl), Pf, Gamba(Vc)ad lib.   Peters
PEZ   Trio Sonata--C.   Fl, Fl(Vl), Vc, Pf.   Ed: Woehl. . . . .   Rieter-B(1938); Peters
PUGNI   Quar.   Fl, Va, Vc, Pf. . . . . . . . . . . . . . .   Ricordi
QUANTZ   Trio Sonata--D.   Ed: Seiffert. . . . . . . . .   Kistner(1935)
                Trio Sonata--F.   Ed: Kint. . . . . . . . . . . .   Zimmerman(1937)
                Trio Sonata--F.   Ed: Leeuwen. . . . . . . . . .   GSch(1928)
STAHL   Nocturno, Op 66.   Hp or Pf. . . . . . . . . . . .   Zimmerman(1897)
STAMITZ   Trio--G, Op 14#1.   Uses Hp.   Ed: Gillman. . . .   Nagel(1933)
                Trio Sonata--F, Op 14#5.   Ed: Hilleman, Coll. Mus. #70 . .   B&H(1938); Andraud
STOELZEL   Sonata, Op 3.   Ed: Frotscher, Coll. Mus#72 . . . . . . . .   B&H(1943)
TELEMANN   Die Kleine Kammermusik, 6 Suites (1716). . . . . . . . . . .
                Trio Sonata--f mi. . . . . . . . . . . . . . . .   Moeck; McG & M
                Trio Sonata--a mi, from Exercicii Musici.   Ed: Woehl. . .   Peters(1938)
                ditto . . . . . . . . . . . . . . . .   Ed: Friedrich   Schott(1938)
                Trio Sonata--c mi.   Fl(Vl), Ob(Vl, Gamba), Pf, Vc.   Ed: Woehl   Peters
                Trio Sonata--c mi.   Fl(Vl), Ob(Vl), Vc(Bn), Pf.
                        Ed: Lauschmann . . . . . .   Forberg
                Quartets;--D, g mi.   Ed: Ermeler.   . . . . . . . . .   Zimmerman(1932)
                Quartets--e mi, b mi.   Ed: Dohrn.   . . . . . . . .   Nagel(1928)
                Sonata a 4--G.   Fl, 2Gamba(Va or Vc & Vc), Pf.
                        Ed: Döbereiner.   . . . . . . . . . .   Schott(1930); AMP
WEISSE   A Queer Kaffeklatsch, Op 32.   Fl, Vl, Cl(Va), Pf. . . . . .   Litolff(1932-33); Andraud


Ob, Vl, Vc, Pf unless otherwise given.

_____   Collegium Musicum.   See Fl, Vl, Vc, Pf
DESHEVOV   Exotic Suite (1935). . . . . . . . . . . . . .   B-N
DUNHILL   Berceuse & Minuet.   Fl(Ob), Vl, Va, Pf. . . . . .   Augener(1937)
GRAUN   Trio Sonata--F.   Ed: Riemann, Coll. Mus#24-26. . . .   B&H(1906); AMP
HANDEL   See 2Ob, Vc, Pf
                Sonatas 1, 2--c mi, F.   Fl(Ob), Vl, Vc, Pf.
                        Ed:  Mönkemeyer . . . . .   Schott(1939)
QUANTZ   Trio Sonata--D.   Fl(Ob), Vl, Vc, Pf.   Ed: Seiffert. . .   Kistner(1935)
STOELZEL   Sonata, Op 3.   Fl(Ob), Vl, Vc, Pf.   Ed: Frotscher.   B&H(1943)
                Trio Sonata--f mi.   2Ob(Vl), Vc, Pf.   Ed: Osthoff.   .   Nagel(1937)
                Sonata--c mi.   2Ob(Vl), Vc(Bn), Pf.   Ed: Frotscher.   Bisping
TELEMANN   Die Kleine Kammermusik, 6 Suites.   Fl(Ob), Vl, Vc, Pf . . . . .


Cl, 2 Str, Pf

BEAUMONT   Suite--G.   With Va, Vc.   . . . . . . . . .   Woolhouse(c1900)
HINDEMITH   Quartet (1938).   With Vl, Vc. . . . . . . . .   Schott(1939); AMP
KAMINSKI   Quar--a mi, Op lb.   With Va, Vc.   . . . . . . .   UE(1926); Andraud
KREUTZER, KONR.   Fantasy on a Swiss Th--Ab, Op 55.   With Va, Vc. . . . . .
MESSIAEN   Quat. pour la fin du temps (1941).   Vl, Vc.   . . . .   Durand; E-V

Cl, 2 Str, Pf cont.

POGGE   Quar--B, Op 7 (1906).   With Vl, Vc.  .. .. .. .. .. .. .. .Author publ. (Kassel)
RABL   Quar--Eb, Op 1.  With Vl, Vc. . . . . . . . . . . Simrock(1897)


Misc.

VELLONES   Rhapsodie, Op 92.  AltSx, Hp, Celeste, Perc.  . . . Lemoine; E-V


## 4 INSTS. : including 2 Winds

2 Winds, Vl, Va

MALIPIERO   Epodi e Giambi.   Ob, Bn. . . . . . . . . . McG & M


2 Winds, Vl, Vc

HONEGGER   Trois Contrepoints (1923).   Picc, Ob(EH).  . . . Hansen(1926)
HYE- KNUDSEN   Quar--a mi, Op 3.  Fl, Ob&EH. . . . . . . Hansen(1926); Andraud
RIISAGER   Serenade, Op 15.  Fl, Cl. . . . . . . . . . . Hansen(1931)
        Sonate, Op 24.  Fl, Cl. . . . . . . . . . . Hansen(1931); Andraud
RAASTED   Serenade--F, Op 40.  Fl, Ob. . . . . . . . . McG & M


2 Winds, Va, Vc

BORODIN   Quartet [orig. for Strs. ?].   Fl, Ob. . . . . . . Leeds
FRÖHLICH   Serenade--A.  Fl, Cl, Va, Vc(Bn).  Ed: Altmann. . Müller(1944)
HOYER   Elegie, 3 voice Canon.  2Fl(Vl), Va, Vc(Bn). . . . . Portius(1937)
MASSARANI   Pastorale.  Ob, Bn. . . . . . . . . . . . . . . . .
MORTARI   3 Antique Dances freely transcr.  Fl, Ob. . . . . Carisch(1937)
MOZART  Andante for Mechanical Organ--F, K 616.
            Arr: Fl, Ob, Va, Vc by Goehr. . . . . . . . Schott; AMP
RAASTED   Serenade--F, Op 40.  Fl, Ob. . . . . . . . . . Kistner & S(1925); Andraud


## 4 INSTS. : including 2 Winds & Pf(Keyboard, etc. )*

2 Fl, Vc, Pf

_____   Collegium Musicum, Collection of nearly 60 17th- & 18th Cent.
            chamber music works.  2Vl(Fl, Ob), Pf, Vc ad lib. . . . . B&H
_____   Masters of the Baroque, Collection of Trio Sonatas.
            Ed. for 2 Fl(Vl), Pf, Vc ad lib. . . . . . . . Peters
BACH, J. S.   Trio Sonata--G.  Ed: Seiffert. . . . . . . . . B&H(1920)
            ditto.  Ed: Landshoff, in Bach Trio Sonaten I . . Peters(1937)
            Trio Sonata--G.  Arr. -- Bb. . . . . . . . . . MBaron


*See remarks in Preface on instrument of Baroque Trio-Sonata editions.

2 Fl, Vc, Pf cont.

BACH, W. FR.   Trio--a mi.   Ed: Seiffert. . . . . . . . .   B&H; AMP, IMC
                Trio Sonata--D.   Ed: Leeuwen. . . . . . . .   Zimmerman(1933); Andraud
FRESCOBALDI   5 Canzoni a 2 canti.   Ed: David. . . . . .   Schott; AMP, MBaron
GEBEL   Triosonaten--F, b mi.   Ed: Seiffert. . . . . . . .   Kistner & S(1926)
HANDEL   See 24 Trio Sonatas under 2Ob, Vc, Pf category.
LEGRENZI   Sonata--d mi (1655). . . . . . . . . . . . .   Peters
LOCATELLI   Trio--G, Op 3#1.   2Vl(Fl), Vc, Pf.   Ed: Riemann .   B&H(1906); AMP, IMC
PAISABLE   Sonatas--d, g, F, c, C; Nr 1-5.   Ed: Friedrich. . . .   Moeck(1939); McG & M
PEZ   Trio Sonate--C.   Ed: Woehl. . . . . . . . . . . .   Rieter-B(1938); Peters
PROWO   Sonatas--g mi, Bb; Nr 5, 6.   Ed: Friedrich. . . . .   Moeck(1940); McG & M #5
TELEMANN   Sonata--A.   Ed: Schreiter. . . . . . . . . .   B&H(1938)
            Quartet--d mi, Tafelmusik II#2.   Ed: Seiffert. . .   B&H(1931)
            Quartet--e mi, Tafelmusik III#2.   Ed: Seiffert. . .   B&H(1928); AMP


2 Ob, Vc, Pf unless otherwise given.

            Collegium Musicum.   See 2Fl, Vc, Pf.
HANDEL   6 Trio Sonatas--Bb, d, Eb, F, G, D; B&H Nr 1-6, no Op Nr.
                2Ob(FL, Vl), Pf, Vc(Bn)ad lib.   Ed: Seiffert. . .   B&H(1906-24)
            ditto   .   . 2Ob, Bs(Pf).   Ed: Krause. . . . .   Schott(c1889-1910)
            9 Trio Sonatas, B&H No 7-15--c, g, F, Bb, F, g, g, g, E; Op 2#1-9.
                2Ob(Fl, Vl), Pf, Vc(Bn)ad lib.   Ed: Seiffert. . .   B&H(c1903-24)
            ditto   .   .   .   Ed: Krause. . . . . .   Schott(1889-1910)
            7 Trio Sonatas, B&H No 16-22--A, D, e, G, g, F, Bb; Op 5#1-7.
                2Ob(Fl, Vl), Pf, Vc(Bn)ad lib.   Ed: Seiffert. . .   B&H(1924)
            Trio Sonata, B&H No 23--g mi; no Op Nr.
                2Ob(Fl, Vl), Pf, Vc(Bn)ad lib.   Ed: Seiffert. . .   B&H(1934)
            Trio Sonata, B&H No 24--F.   Ob, Bn, Vc, Pf[Inst ?]*
                                Ed: Seiffert. . .   B&H(1938)
            2 Trio Sonatas--c mi, g mi; Op 2#1, 2.   2Ob(Fl, Vl), Pf, Vc
                ad lib.   Ed: Peyrot, Rebuffat. . . . . .   Senart(1911); IMC #2
            Trio Sonata--Eb, Op 2#3.   2Fl(Ob), Bs(Pf).
                                Ed: Schikkel . . . . . .   Heugel(1924)
PAISABLE   Sonatas--d, g, F, c, C; Nr 1-5.   2Fl(Ob, Vl), Pf, Vc ad lib.
                                Ed: Friedrich. . . . .   Moeck(1939); McG & M
PROWO   Sonatas--g mi, Bb; Nr 5, 6.   2 Fl(Ob), Pf, Vc ad lib.
                                Ed: Friedrich. . . . .   Moeck(1940); McG & M #5
STOELZEL   Trio Sonate--f mi.   Ed: Osthoff. . . . . . . .   Nagel(1937)
            Sonata--c mi.   Vc or Bn.   Ed: Frotscher. . . .   Bisping
UCCELLINI   Wedding of Hen & Cuckoo.   2Ob(Cl), Vc(Bn), Pf.
                        Ed: Lenzewski, Sr. . . . . . . . .   Vieweg(1930); Andraud


Misc. :   2 Winds, 1 Str, Pf(Hp)

CASELLA   Sinfonia, Op 54.   Cl, Tt, Vc, Pf. . . . . . . . .   Carisch(1931); Andraud
CASTERA   Concerto--A (1911-22).   Fl, Cl(Vl), Vc, Pf. . . . .   Rouart(1924); Andraud
DOPPLER   Nocturne, Op 19.   Fl, Vl, Hn(Vc), Pf. . . . . . . .   Schott; Andraud
GRIMM, C. H.   Fantasia--d mi.   2Cl, Vc, Pf. . . . . . . . . . .
MIGOT   Quartet.   Fl(Vl), Vl, Cl(Va), Hp. . . . . . . . . .   SireneM(1927); Andraud
MILLAULT   Sonatine--F.   Fl, Cl, Vl, Pf. . . . . . . . . .   Lemoine(1880)

_____
*The instrumentation given is unlikely.

Misc: 2 Winds, 1Str, Pf(Hp) cont.

OLENIN    Preludes prairiales.  2Ob, Vl, Pf.  . . . . . . . . .  B-N
PEPUSCH   Trio Sonata--g mi.  Fl, Ob(Vl), Pf, Gamba(Vc)ad lib..  Peters
REICHA    Quartet, Op 104.  Fl, Vc, Bn, Pf.  . . . . . . . . . . . . . .
REINSTEIN   Music for --Eb, Op 34.  Fl, Cl, Vl, Pf.  . . . . .  Litolff(1933); Andraud
SOURILAS   Suite--F.  Ob, Hn, Vc, Hp.  . . . . . . . . . . .  Lemoine(1899); B-N
STARER   Concertino.  Ob, Tb, Vl, Pf.  . . . . . . . . . .  Ms available Juilliard
TELEMANN   Sonata--F.  Fl, Ob, Pf, Vc ad lib.   Ed: Rodemann.  Moeck(1939); McG & M
            Trio--c mi.  Fl(Vl), Ob(Vl), Pf, Vc(Bn)ad lib.
                  Ed: Lauschmann. . . . . . . . . .  Forbert(1925)
            Trio Sonata--c mi.  Fl(Vl), Ob(Vl, Gamba), Pf, Vc ad lib.   Ed: Woehl. . Peters
            Trio--e mi, Tafelmusik II.  Ob, Fl, Pf, Vc ad lib.
                  Ed: Seiffert, Coll. Mus#55.  . . . .  B&H; AMP
WEBERN   Quartet, Op 22.  Vl, Cl, TenSx, Pf.  . . . . . . . .  UE(1932)
WEISSE   A Queer Kaffeklatsch, Op 32.  Fl, Vl, Cl(Va), Pf. . . .  Litolff(1932-33); Andraud
ZACHOW   Trio--F.  Fl(Ob), Bn, Pf, Vc ad lib.   Ed: Seiffert.  .  Kistner(1929)

## 4 INSTS. : including 3 Winds

BACH, K. P. E.   March Fanfare.  3Tt, Tymp. . . . . . . . .  Marks
DESSAU   Concertino.  Solo Vl, Fl, Cl, Hn.  . . . . . . . .  Schott; AMP
ETLER   Quartet.  Ob, Cl, Va, Bn. . . . . . . . . . . .  Valley
FRÖHLICH   Serenade --A.  Fl, Cl, Va, Vc(Bn).  Ed: Altmann.  .  W. Müller(1949)
HOYER   Elegie, 3 voice Canon.  2Fl(Vl), Va, Vc(Bn). . . . .  Portius(1937)
VILLA-LOBOS   Choros #6.  Cl, Tt, Bombardine, Guitar.  . . . . . .
WECKMANN   8 Sonatas.  Cornettino, Vl, Tb, Bn.   Ed: Ilgner,
                  in Erbe dt. Musik.  . . .  Litolff(1942)

## 4 INSTS. : including 3 Winds & Pf(Keyboard, etc. )

3 Fl, Pf

COLBY   Three Blind Mice, Scherzo.  3Cl(Fl), Pf ad lib.  . .  Remick; MPHC
KRAKAMP   Scherzo, Op 100. . . . . . . . . . . . . . .  B-N
RORICH   Burleske--a mi, Op 64. . . . . . . . . . . . . .  Zimmerman(1922); B-N
TELEMANN   See 3Fl, Pf, Vc ad lib.

3 Brass, Pf(Organ)

CLOUGH   The Three Trombonists.  3Tb, Pf.  . . . . . . .  Boosey(1923)
LASSUS   Providebam Dominum.  3Ct, Organ.  . . . . . .  Mus f Brass
SARTORIUS   Trumpet Threesome.  3Ct(Tt), Pf. . . . . . . .  Merc

Fl, Ob, Cl, Pf

AMBERG   Suite--Bb. . . . . . . . . . . . . . . . . .  Hansen(1905); Andraud
CAVALLINI   Trio--F. . . . . . . . . . . . . . . . . .  Ricordi(1890); Andraud
EHRHART   Alsatian Waltzes, 2 Suites, Op 20. . . . . . .  Andraud
FRANCAIX   Quartet. . . . . . . . . . . . . . . . . .  Andraud
HAMM   Triologue.  . . . . . . . . . . . . . . . . .  B-N

Fl, Ob, Cl, Pf cont.

MARIOTTE   On the Mt.   Fl(Ob), Cl, EH(Bn), Pf. . . . . . . . Andraud
MAYEUR   Trio. . . . . . . . . . . . . . . . . . . . . B-N
MILHAUD   Sonate (1918). . . . . . . . . . . . . . . . Durand(1923); E-V
PAGANINI   Perpetual Motion.   Arr: Tustin. . . . . . . . Spratt
SAINT-SAENS   Caprice on Danish & Russ. Airs--Bb, Op 79 . . Durand; E-V


2 Ob, Bn, Pf*

HANDEL   Trio Sonatas, B&H Nr 1-23.   See 20b, Vc, Pf category.
          Trio Sonata--Eb, Op 1#3 (1696)** . . . . . . . . . Merc
STOELZEL   Sonata--c mi.   Ed: Frotscher. . . . . . . . . Bisping
UCCELLINI   Wedding of Hen & Cuckoo.   20b(Cl), Vc(Bn), Pf.
                    Ed: Lenzewski, Sr. . . . . . . . Vieweg(1930); Andraud


Misc.

BACH, J. S.   Trio Sonata--G.   Arr: 2Fl, Pf, Vc(Bn)ad lib. --Bb.  MBaron
BRUNEAU   Quartet.   Fl, Ob, Hn, Pf. . . . . . . . . . . Peregally(Paris, 1902)
COLBY   Three Blind Mice, Scherzo--Eb.   3Cl(Fl), Pf ad lib. .  Remick; MPHC
FRESCOBALDI   5 Canzoni a 2 canti.   2Fl(Vl), Pf, Vc(Bn)ad lib.
          Ed: H. David. . . . . . . . . . . . . . Schott; AMP, MBaron
GRUNENWALD   Fantaisie Arabesque.   Ob, Cl, Bn, Pf. . . . . . MBaron
HONEGGER   Rhapsody--c mi (1917).   2Fl, Cl, Pf. . . . . . . Senart(1923); Andraud
KARG-ELERT   Youth--B, Op 139a.   Fl, Cl, Hn, Pf. . . . . . Zimmerman(1924); Andraud
MARIOTTE   On the Mt.   Fl(Ob, Cl, EH(Bn), Pf. . . . . . . Andraud
MOZART   German Dance--a mi.   Fl(Vl), Ob(Vl), Bn(Vc), Pf  ad lib. .  Peters
RIETI   Sonata.   Fl, Ob, Bn, Pf. . . . . . . . . . . . . . UE(1926); Andraud
ROLAND-MANUEL   Suite dans le gout espagnol (1939?).
                    Ob, Bn, Tt, Pf. . . . . . . Durand(1941); E-V
RÜDIGER   Sinf. Intermezzo.   Fl(Ob), Cl, Bn, Pf. . . . . . Author publ. (Weimar, 1932)
SCHERBER   Quartet--Bb.   Ob, Cl, BsCl, Pf. . . . . . . . Schmidt(1914); Andraud
SCHMITT   A tour d'anches, Op 97.   Ob, Cl, Bn, Pf. . . . . . Durand; E-V
WEISMANN   Divertimento, Op 38.   Cl, Bn, Hn, Pf. . . . . . . . . . . .


4  INSTS. :  4 Similar Woodwinds


4 Fl

_____   3 & 4 Pt. Canons & Rounds. . . . . . . . . . . . Merc
_____   2 Sets of "Curiosities. "   Ed: Leeuwen. . . . . . . Remick; MPHC
_____   4 Miniatures, pcs. by Mozart, Bohm, Tsch. , Rimsky-K.
                    Arr: Leeuwen. . . . . . . . . . Andraud, MBaron
BECKERATH   Quartet. . . . . . . . . . . . . . . . . . Moeck(1939)
BENNETT   Rondo capriccioso. . . . . . . . . . . . . . N. Y. Flute Club(1922); B-N
CLINTON   Quar--G, Op 32. . . . . . . . . . . . . . . Ashdown

_____

*See remarks in Preface on instrumentation of Baroque Trio-Sonata editions.
**The Op 1 Sonatas are Solo Sonatas.  If this instrumentation, and Opus is correct, it is a most
unusual realization of the music.

## 4 Fl cont.

COHEN, (S. B. ?)  Colonial Sketches. . . . . . . . . . . Boosey
DESPORTES  Italian Suite. . . . . . . . . . . . . . . . Andraud
FARRENC  Andante.  Arr; 3Fl, AltFl in G(Cl) by Brooke . . . C-B
FÜRSTENAU  Quar--F, Op 88. . . . . . . . . . . . . . Ashdown; B-N
GABRIELSKI  3 Quar--G, A, e mi; Op 53. . . . . . . . . B&H; AMP
GUILLEMAIN, (L. G. ?)  Tambourin.  Arr; Taylor. . . . . Mills
HERRMANN, HUGO  Quar. . . . . . . . . . . . . . . . Bote & Bock(1931)
JONGEN  Elegy. . . . . . . . . . . . . . . . . . . . Andraud
KÖHLER  Quar--D, Op 92. . . . . . . . . . . . . . . Zimmerman(1904); B-N
KUHLAU  Quar--e mi, Op 103. . . . . . . . . . . . . Richault; B-N, MBaron
KUNTZ  Kleine Passacaglia. . . . . . . . . . . . . . Moeck(1941)
LAUBER  Visions de Corse. . . . . . . . . . . . . . Zimmerman(1937)
LEEUWEN  Var. on Turkey in the Straw. . . . . . . . . Andraud
LORENZO  Followers of Pan, Op 32. . . . . . . . . . Zimmerman(1930); B-N
MAGANINI  Realm of Dolls, Op 9 (1922). . . . . . . . . CFisch(1923)
MARX  Kleine Suite after L. Mozart's Notebook.  Also other insts. . . . . Hanseat(1939)
McKAY, (G. F. ?)  Christmas Morning. . . . . . . . . Andraud
PIZZI  Divertissement. . . . . . . . . . . . . . . . Ricordi
REICHA  Quar--D, Op 12. . . . . . . . . . . . . . . Hofmeister(1861); C-B, B-N
SCHMITT  Quartet, Op 106. . . . . . . . . . . . . . Durand; E-V
SOUSSMANN  Quar--D, Op 5. . . . . . . . . . . . . Lischke(Berlin)
                Quar--G, C; Op 27#1, 2. . . . . . . . . . Schuberth(Leipzig)
TURECHEK  See 4Fl, Pf.
WALCKIERS  Quar--F, Op 70. . . . . . . . . . . . . Ashdown
                Quar--f# mi, Op 46. . . . . . . . . . . . Zimmerman(1923); B-N
                Rondo.  Arr: 3Fl, AltFl(Cl) by Brooke. . . . . . C-B, B-N
WINSLOE  Fluteplayer's Serenade. . . . . . . . . . . Belwin
WOUTERS  Scherzo & Adagio-g mi, Eb; Op 77. . . . . . . . Oertel(Brussels, 1889); B-N

## 4 Cl

_____  3 & 4 Pt. Canons & Rounds. . . . . . . . . . . Merc
ARTOT, A. J.  12 Quar.  Arr: Harris. . . . . . . . . C-B
BACH, J. S.  Bach for the Clarinet.  Arr: Simon. . . . . . GSch
                Fugue #16--g mi.  Arr: 2Cl, Cl(AltCl), Cl(BsCl) by Pentz . . Belwin
BALAY  Sarabande & Menuet from Petite Suite.  Arr:
                2Cl, AltCl(Cl), BsCl by Waln. . . . . . . . . . . Kjos
BEETHOVEN  Andante Cantabile from Symph I.  Arr: 4Cl or
                ClQuar by Geiger. . . . . . . . . . . . . . Remick; MPHC
                Allegro con brio from StrQuar--F, Op 18#1.
                Arr: ClQuar--Eb by Wilson. . . . . . . . . : . CFisch(1948)
                Scherzo from Sonata for Pf--Ab, Op 26.  Arr:
                ClQuar by Harris. . . . . . . . . . . . . . Gornston
BOHNE, (R?)  Andante from Quar--D.  Arr: 4Cl or ClQuar by Voxman. . Rubank
BOROWSKI  Whimsies. . . . . . . . . . . . . . . . . Belwin
BOZZA  Andante & Scherzo. . . . . . . . . . . . . . Andraud
COHEN, (S. B. ?)  Alabama Sketches. . . . . . . . . . . Witmark; MPHC
CROSSE  Suite. . . . . . . . . . . . . . . . . . . Boosey(1906)
DEBUSSY  Nocturne; Reverie.  Arr: ClQuar by Howland . . . Schmitt
DESPORTES  Normandie, Suite on Ancient Airs. . . . . . . Andraud
                French Suite. . . . . . . . . . . . . . . MBaron
DONT  Larghetto & Scherzo.  Arr: Waln. . . . . . . . . Kjos

## 4 Cl cont.

FOGELBERG   Danza.   4Cl or ClQuar. . . . . . . . . . . Remick; MPHC
GABRIELSKI   Grand Quartet, Op 53#5. . . . . . . . . . MBaron
GOEB   Suite in Folk Style. . . . . . . . . . . . . . Broadcast; AMP
KRENEK   Country Dance. . . . . . . . . . . . . . . Belwin
LEFEBVRE   Intermezzo from 2nd Suite, Op 122.  Arr: Waln. . . . . Kjos
            Prelude from 2nd Suite, Op 122.  Arr: Waln for ClQuar . . . Kjos
MAYEUR, (L?)   1st Quar.  Arr: ClQuar by Voxman. . . . . . . . . Rubank
MENDELSSOHN, (F?).  Rondo Capriccioso.  Arr: ClQuar by Howland . . . . Schmitt
MOZART   Adagio from Cl Concerto--A, K 622 (1791).  Arr: ClQuar by Laube . . C-B
MÜLLER, IWAN   3 Quartets. . . . . . . . . . . . . . . . . .
POWELL   Quartet (1936).  ClQuar. . . . . . . . . . CFisch(1938)
SCARLATTI, D.   Pastorale.  Arr: 4Cl or ClQuar by Wilson. . Remick; MPHC
SCHUMANN   Scherzo of Quar--a mi, Op 41#1 (1842).  Arr:
                        ClQuar by Howland.   . . . Selmer
SKINNER   Scherzetto; Capricietta. . . . . . . . . . . Belwin
SPOHR   Concerto #1.   Arr: 3Cl, Bn or ClQuar by Tallmadge. . Remick; MPHC
STAMITZ   Andante.  Arr: 4Cl or ClQuar. . . . . . . . C-B
TELEMANN   Concerto.  Arr. . . . . . . . . . . . . . Marks
THOMSON   Five Portraits (1929). . . . . . . . . . . . . . . . . .
WATERSON   Grand Quartet. . . . . . . . . . . . . Mahillon(1886); MBaron

## 4 Bn

DUBENSKY   Prelude & Fugue (1933). . . . . . . . . . . Ricordi
PROKOVIEV   Scherzo humoristique.  . . . . . . . . . Russ. M-V(c1938); MBaron
SCHUMAN, WM.   Quartettino (1939). . . . . . . . . . Boletin Latino-Americano(1941)

## 4 Sx

          3 & 4 Pt. Canons & Rounds. . . . . . . . . . . Merc
BORMANN   Suite im alten Stil. . . . . . . . . . . . . Frölich(1941)
BOZZA   Andante & Scherzo.   4Cl(Sx). . . . . . . . . Andraud
          Nuages.   SopSx, AltSx, TenSx, BarSx. . . . . . . . MBaron
BUMCKE   2 Quar, Op 23. . . . . . . . . . . . . . Diem(1908)
CARTER   Suite (1942).   4AltSx. . . . . . . . . . . . . Broadcast; AMP, MBaron
CLARISSE   Chanson de Romet; Intro. & Scherzo; Serenade Melancolique . . . . . . . . .
          Caravane. . . . . . . . . . . . . Buffet-Crampon(1937)
COHEN   Novelette.  SxQuar. . . . . . . . . . . . Belwin
DUPERIER   Trios airs pour un soir de mai. . . . . . . . . Lemoine(1936)
FRANCAIX   Petit Quatuor.  SopSx, AltSx, TenSx, BarSx. . . . Schott(1939); AMP
HAUBIEL, (CHAS. ?)   For Louis XVI.  SxQuar. . . . . . . Belwin
JONGEN   Quartet (1942). . . . . . . . . . . . . . .
LOUP   Pavane a un herôs disparu. . . . . . . . . . . Leduc(1939)
MIELENZ   Scherzo.  Arr: SxQuar by Voxman. . . . . . . . Rubank
MORITZ, EDV.   Andante.  SxQuar. . . . . . . . . . Merc

**4 Sx** cont.

| | | |
|---|---|---|
| PIERNE, GABR. | Intro & Var sur une ronde populaire . . . . . | Leduc(1939); MBaron |
| | March of Little Lead Soldiers. | |
| |     Arr: SopSx, AltSx, TenSx, BarSx by Mule. . . | MBaron |
| | La Veilee de l'ange gardien. | |
| |     SopSx, AltSx, TenSx, BarSx. . . . . | MBaron |
| PIERNE, PAUL | Trois Conversations. . . . . . . . . . | Costallat(1943); MBaron |
| RAMSOE | Quar #5, 1st mvt. Arr: SxQuar by Voxman. . . . | Rubank |
| SCHMITT | Quatuor en 4 parties, Op 102. . . . . . . . | Durand; E-V |
| SCHMUTZ | Prelude & Finale. 2AltSx, TenSx, Ten(Bar)Sx. . . | AMP; MBaron |
| | Intro., Recitative & Chorale. SxQuar or 2AltSx, 2TenSx. . . | AMP |
| SINGELIE | Allegro de Concert. SxQuar. . . . . . . . | CFisch |
| THOU | Suite. . . . . . . . . . . . . . . | Fröhlich(1941) |

## 4 INSTS. : 4 Mixed Woodwinds

**W.W. Quar: Fl, Ob(EH), Cl, Bn**

| | | |
|---|---|---|
| _____ | Quartet on Old Tunes. Arr: Sontag. . . . . . . | Presser |
| ALBISI | Divertimento #3. . . . . . . . . . . | Andraud |
| ARTOT, A.J. | 12 Quar. Arr: Harris. . . . . . . . . | C-B |
| BACH, J.S. | Fughetta. Arr: Cafarella. . . . . . . . | Witmark; MPHC |
| | Prelude & Fugue #14, W.T.C. Arr: Kessler . . | Rubank |
| BERGER, ART. | Quar--C (1941). . . . . . . . . . . | Arrow |
| BRIDGE | Divertimenti. . . . . . . . . . . . | Boosey |
| DAHLHOFF | Sumpf, Dramatic Dance Scene. . . . . . . | Schmidt(1925); Andraud |
| DANZI | Gypsy Dance. Arr: Maganini. . . . . . . | CFisch |
| DELAMARTER | Sketch Book in Eire. . . . . . . . . | Andraud |
| DESORMIERE | 6 16th-Cent. Danceries. Fl, EH, Cl, Bn. . . . | MBaron |
| DURAND | Chaconne, Op 62. . . . . . . . . . | Presser |
| EGIDI | Quar, Op 19. . . . . . . . . . . . | Wölbing(1925); Andraud |
| FERNANDEZ | Suite--F, Op 37#2. . . . . . . . . | AMP |
| FINNEY | Ballabile. . . . . . . . . . . . | Witmark; MPHC |
| GERMAN | Pastoral Dance. . . . . . . . . . | CFisch |
| GOEPFART | Quar--d mi, Op 93. . . . . . . . . | F. Schuberth(1907); Andraud |
| HOLBROOKE | Quar--Db, Op 94. . . . . . . . . . | Mod. Mus. Libr. (1932); Andraud |
| HUGUES | Quar--g mi, Op 72. . . . . . . . . | Ricordi |
| | Quar--b mi, Op 76. . . . . . . . . | Ricordi |
| KABALEVSKY | Childrens Suite, Op 27. Arr: Seay. . . . . | Spratt |
| LAUBER | 4 Intermezzi. Fl, EH, Cl, Bn. . . . . . . | Henn(1922); Andraud |
| MELKIKH | Quar, Op 19. . . . . . . . . . . | |
| MIELENZ | Scherzo. Fl, EH, Cl, Bn. . . . . . . | Wilke(1938-40) |
| MOZART | Adagio. Arr: Richter. . . . . . . . | Remick; MPHC |
| PAGANINI | LaChasse. Arr: Vognar. . . . . . . | Remick; MPHC |
| PAQUIS | 3 Quar--F, G, F; Op 1. . . . . . . . . | Costallat |
| PIRANI | Gavotte Rococo, Whirlwind. . . . . . . | |
| PROKOVIEV | 2 Visions Fugitives. . . . . . . . . | Andraud |
| PROVINCIALI | Danse Villageoise. . . . . . . . . | Eschig; AMP, MBaron |
| RAKOV | 3 Miniatures. Fl, Ob(EH), Cl, Bn. . . . . . | Leeds |
| RIEGGER | 3 Canons, Op 9 (1931). . . . . . . . | NME V#4(1932) |
| SCHUBERT, FR. | Minuet. Arr: Cafarella. . . . . . . . | Witmark; MPHC |

W. W. Quar: Fl, Ob(EH), Cl, Bn  cont.

SCHUMANN, ROBT.   Scenes from Childhood, Op 15 (1838) .
                                         Arr: Gillette . . . . . .  Witmark; MPHC
SCHWARTZ   Evening in the Turkestan Stepp.  Fl, EH(Ob), Cl, Bn. Hawkes(1937)
SHAW   For the Gentlemen (Publ. 1807).  Arr. . . . . . . . .  Merc
TURECHEK   Divertissement--f mi.   . . . . . . . . . . .  Witmark; MPHC
TUTHILL   Divertimento Classic Style, Op 14#2 (1936). . . . .  CFisch(1938); Andraud
VALENTINI   Quartettino.  . . . . . . . . . . . . . .  Author publ. (Modena, 1933)
WUILLEUMIER   Prelude, Gavott, Canon, Mazurka.  Fl,EH,Cl,Bn. . Andraud


Fl, Ob, Hn, Bn

HAYDN, MICH.   Divertimento--D.  Ed: Lauschmann.  . . . .  Hofmeister(1931)
HERMANN, FR.   Collection of Str Ensemble transcriptions, Bk I. . B&H(1899)


Fl, Cl, Hn, Bn

DÜRING   Quar. . . . . . . . . . . . . . . . . . . . .  Hedler(Frankf't a/M, 1845)
HÄNSEL, P.   3 Quar. . . . . . . . . . . . . . . . . . . . . . . . . . .
KREJCI   Divertimento.  . . . . . . . . . . . . . .  Hudebni Matice(1927); Andraud
MELCHOIR, A. J. B.   Quar #6--G. . . . . . . . . . .  Costallat
                     Quar, Op 8. . . . . . . . . . .  Lemoine
                     Quar, Op 1. . . . . . . . . . .  Lemoine
                     Quar--d mi, Op 20. . . . . . . .  Costallat
MENGAL   6 Quar, Op 18, 19. . . . . . . . . . . . . .  Lemoine
ROSSINI   Quar--F. . . . . . . . . . . . . . . . . .  Merc
          6 Quar.  Arr: Zachert.  (Only 1 orig. for winds). . .  Schott(1936); AMP
SCHAFFNER   3 Quar--F, d mi, C; Op 5. . . . . . . . . .  B&H
STRINGFIELD   An Old Bridge.  Ob(Fl), Cl, Hn(EH), Bn. . . . .  Leeds
WALCKIERS   3 Quar--Bb, A, F; Op 7. . . . . . . . . . .  Costallat(c1820)
            Quar--Bb, Op 48.  . . . . . . . . . . . .  Schlesinger
            Quar--c mi, Op 73. . . . . . . . . . . .  B&H


Ob, Cl, Hn, Bn

BECHER   Heiteres Quartet--Bb. . . . . . . . . . . . .  Lausch & Zweigle(1933)
KRÜGER   Ein lustiges Quartett. . . . . . . . . . . . .  Ehrler(1934)
LANGE, HANS   Serenade, Op 45. . . . . . . . . . . . .  Author publ. (Berlin, 1942)
MOZART   Cassation.   K ? . . . . . . . . . . . . . . .  MBaron
SCHROTER   Foolish Fantasy. . . . . . . . . . . . . . .  Andraud
STAMITZ   Quar--Eb, Op 8#2.  Arr: Weigelt. . . . . . . .  Leuckart
STRINGFIELD   An Old Bridge. . . . . . . . . . . . . .  Leeds
WETZEL   Humorous Serenade. . . . . . . . . . . . . .  Oertel; Andraud


4  INSTS. : 4 Similar Brass


4 Hn

ANTOINE   Quar, Op 52. . . . . . . . . . . . . . . . . .  Edit. Vienna(1929)
ARTOT, J. D.   12 Quar. . . . . . . . . . . . . . . . .  Schott(1875)

## 4 Hn cont.

BACH, J. S.   Prelude, Fugue & Allegro.   Arr: Treat.  . . . . Witmark; MPHC
BANTOCK   Serenade (1903). . . . . . . . . . . . . . . . . . .
BECK   Quar, Op 1. . ... . . . . . . . . . . . . . . . . . . Gries & Schornagel(1909)
CHAVEZ   Sonata. . . . . . . . . . . . . . . . . . . . . . . .
DAUPRAT   6 Trios & 6 Quar, Op 8. . . . . . . . . . . Lemoine(c1840)
DIEWITZ   Quar. . . . . . . . . . . . . . . . . . . . . Hofmeister(1926)
GUMBERT, (FR. ?)   Quartet Collection, 4 Bks. . . . . . . . . Hofmeister(1877-78)
HÄNSEL, AUG.   7 Original Quar, Op 75. . . . . . . . . . Hofmeister(1859)
HOLZNER   Der Heide Ruf. . . . . . . . . . . . . . . Author publ. (Leipzig, 1943)
HOMILIUS   Quar--Bb, Op 38. . . . . . . . . . . . . . Hofmeister(1893)
KIENZL   3 Konzertstücke, Op 108. . . . . . . . . . . . Oertel(1926)
KRAUSE   Am Festmorgen, 3 mvts. . . . . . . . . . . . L. Hoffman(1887)
KRONKE   Chanson; Caprice; Op 60. . . . . . . . . . . Schott(1911)
LIFTL   Suite, Op 185. . . . . . . . . . . . . . . . . Schmidt(1927); MBaron
MÜLLER, BERNH.   Orig. Quar #1-12 (1889), #13-18 (1907). . . Zimmerman(1907)
OTEY   Symphonic Sketches. . . . . . . . . . . . . . . Andraud, MBaron
          Prelude, Scherzo, Passacaglia. . . . . . . . . . . Sansone
OTTO   Quar, Op 107.   Ed: Gumbert. . . . . . . . . . . Hofmeister(1897)
PAEPKE   Suite, Op 6. . . . . . . . . . . . . . . . . . Böhm(1938)
PERILHOU   Chasse. . . . . . . . . . . . . . . . . . . Heugel(c1902); Merc
POTTAG   Quar on motives by Wagner. . . . . . . . . . Belwin
PRÄGER, PAUL   2 Quar, Op 151, 155. . . . . . . . . . Rob. Rühle(1939, 1936)
REICHA   Quar--D, Op 12.   [Arr. ?]. . . . . . . . . . Hamelle(1861)
RUMMEL   2 Sets of 6 Quar; Op 60b, 69b. . . . . . . . . Schott(bef. 1840)
SCHEIN   Banchetto Musicale Suite #22.   Ed: Prüfer. . . . . . B&H(1903); AMP
STRONG   Legend. . . . . . . . . . . . . . . . . . . . Henn(Geneva, 1913)
SÜSSMUTH   Suite, Op 32. . . . . . . . . . . . . . . . B&H(1938)
SUTTNER   4 Waldhorn Quar. . . . . . . . . . . . . . . Grosch(1942)
TCHEREPNIN   6 Quar. . . . . . . . . . . . . . . . . . Jurgenson(1910)
          Suite.   Ed: Philipp. . . . . . . . . . . . . Belaiev(1937); AMP
WILL   Treue-Gelöbnis, Op 49. . . . . . . . . . . . . . W. Will(Hamburg, 1942)
WINDSPERGER   3 Suites, Op 31. . . . . . . . . . . . . (in Ms) Schott

## 4 Tt(Ct)

FITZGERALD   Caprice. . . . . . . . . . . . . . . . . . Belwin
MOHAUPT   Partita. . . . . . . . . . . . . . . . . . . ABC Music

## 4 Tb

            24 Early German Chorales.   Ed: King. . . . . . . Mus f Brass
BACH, J. S.   16 Chorales.   Arr: King. . . . . . . . . . Mus f Brass
            2 Fugues.   Arr: Rochut. . . . . . . . . . . MBaron
BEETHOVEN   3 Funeral Equali (1912).   Sop, Alt, Ten, BsTb. . . B&H; AMP
BRUNS   21 Quar. . . . . . . . . . . . . . . . . . . . Oertel(1934)
CLAPP   4 mvts. from Concert Suite for Tbs. (1938). . . . . . Boosey
COLBY   Allegro con brio. . . . . . . . . . . . . . . . Remick; MPHC
HAUBIEL, (CHAS?)   Clasici, Romantico, Moderni. . . . . . Belwin
MAAS   2 Quar--Bb, f mi.   Ed: Bruns . . . . . . . . . . Oertel(1920)
MacKAY   Intermezzo. . . . . . . . . . . . . . . . . . Gamble
MÜLLER, R.   50 Quar, 2 Bks. . . . . . . . . . . . . . Hofmeister(1887)
PURCELL   March & Canzona (1695). . . . . . . . . . . . . . .
SANDERS   Scherzo & Dirge. . . . . . . . . . . . . . . AMP
WOYRSCH   Mors triumphans, Op 58 (1915). . . . . . . . . Oertel(1925)

## 2 Tt(Ct), Hn, Tb

BANCHIERI   2 Fantasias.   2Tt, Tb(Hn), Tb(Bar).   Ed: ?  . . .  Merc, MBaron
BOROWSKY   Morning Song. . . . . . . . . . . . . . . .  Boosey
COHEN   Quar for Brass Insts. . . . . . . . . . . . . .  Belwin
FITZGERALD   Tarantella.   2Tt, Tb(Hn), Tb. . . . . . . . .  Belwin
MÜLLER, BERNH.   Kaiser-Quar.   2Ct, BsTt(Eb AltHn),TenHn(Tb).
                                        2 Bks.  . . .  Hofmeister
PARRIS   7 Moods for Brass Quar. . . . . . . . . . . . .  E-V
ROBERDAY   Caprice--F.   2Tt(Ct), Tb(Hn), Tb(Bar).   Ed:?  . .  Merc
SIMON   Sonatina-Quar--Bb, Op 23#1. . . . . . . . . . .  Jurgenson(1890); B-N


## 2 Tt(Ct), Tb, Bar

BANCHIERI    2 Fantasias.   2Tt, Tb(Hn), Tb(Bar).   Ed: ?  . . .  Merc, MBaron
BERGSMA   Suite for Brass Quar (1940). . . . . . . . . . .  CFisch
CAZDEN   Three Directions. . . . . . . . . . . . . . . .  AMP
FRACKENPOHL   Quar. . . . . . . . . . . . . . . . . . .  Mus f Brass
GABRIELI   Canzon Septimi Toni #1.   Ct(Tt), Ct(Hn), Tb, Tb(Bar).  Merc
HAINES   Toccata. . . . . . . . . . . . . . . . . . . .  Mus f Brass
RAMSOE   Quar #3, 4, 5.   2Ct, Hn(Tb), Bar.   Ed: King.  . . .  Mus f Brass
ROBERDAY   Caprice--F.   2Tt, Tb(Hn), Tb(Bar).   Ed: ?  . . .  Merc


## 2 Tt(Ct), 2 Tb

BACH, J. S.   Prelude & Fugue from Klavier Sonata--D.  Arr: ?.  Marks
                Fervent is My Longing.  Arr: Caillet. . . . . .  Belwin(1942)
BANCHIERI   2 Fantasias.   Ed: ? . . . . . . . . . . . .  Merc, MBaron
CAZDEN   Three Directions.   2Ct(Tt), Bar(Tb), Tb. . . . . .  AMP
COLERIDGE-TAYLOR,  Demande et Response . . . . . . . .  Boosey
FITZGERALD   Tarantella. . . . . . . . . . . . . . . . .  Belwin
GABRIELI   Canzon Septimi Toni #1.   Ed:? . . . . . . . . .  Merc
GLAZOUNOV   In Modo Religioso--Eb, Op 38.   Tt, Hn(Tt), 2Tb. .  Marks
HINDEMITH   Morgenmusik from "Plöner Musiktag. "
                     Brass Choir (2Tt, 2Tb). . . . . .  Schott; AMP
KLEIN   Sonata. . . . . . . . . . . . . . . . . . . . .  AMP
REICHA   Hunting Scene. . . . . . . . . . . . . . . . .  MBaron
ROBERDAY   Caprice--F. . . . . . . . . . . . . . . . .  Merc
SCHEIN   Intrada & Paduana. . . . . . . . . . . . . . .  Merc, MBaron
TANEIEV   Rome at Night. . . . . . . . . . . . . . . . .  MBaron
WEBER, LUDW.   Kleine Musik. . . . . . . . . . . . . .  Filser(1930)


## 4 Misc. Brass

        See also listings under 5 Brass.
BACH, J. S.   22 Chorales.  Arr: Ct, Hn, Tb, Bar by King.  . . .  Mus f Brass
BEETHOVEN   3 Funeral Equali (1812) for 4 Tb.
                     Arr: Tt, 3Tb by Kahn. . . . .  Marks
COLBY   Allegro con brio.   3Tb, Tb(Bar). . . . . . . . . .  Remick; MPHC
DUBENSKY   Concerto Grosso.   3Tb, Tuba.  (Orch acc. on hire). Ricordi
MacKAY   Adagio assai & Allegro Vivace. . . . . . . . . .  Gamble
            2 Brass Quar, Op 11, 12. . . . . . . . . . . .  Gamble

**4 Misc. Brass** cont.

RAMSOE   4 Quar--F, Bb, E, Ab; Op 20, 29, 30, 37.   Ct, Tt, TenHn, Tuba.   . . .   Hansen(1888)
    Quar, Op 38.   2Ct, AltHn, Tuba. . . . . . . . . . . . . . . .   Hansen(1888)
    Quar #3, 4, 5.   Arr: 2Ct, Hn(Tb), Bar by King.   . . . . . . . . .   Mus f Brass
REICHE   Turm-Sonate--c mi.   Ct, 3Tb; in Schering Beispielen.   . . . . . .   B&H
    Sonate #19.   Ed: Ct, Tb(Hn), Bar, Tuba by King. . . . . . . . .   Mus f Brass
SCHULZE   50 Quar.   2Hn, TenHn, Tb.   . . . . . . . . . . . . . .   Erdmann(1908)
SPEER   Sonatas--C.G.   Zink(Tt), 3Tb.   Ed: Schultz, Erbe dt. Mus.   . . . . .   Nagel
STÖRL   6 Sonatas.   Zink, AltTb, TenTb, BsTb.   Ed: Schultz, Erbe dt. Mus. . .   Nagel
VILLA-LOBOS   Choros #4.   3Hn, Tb. . . . . . . . . . . .   Schott(1929)

## 4 INSTS. : 4 Misc. Winds

_____   Fugenbüchlein.   Various wind Quar.   Ed: Doflein. . .   Bärenreiter(1936)
_____   Several pcs. arr: Ob, Ob(Cl), Bn(Cl), Bn by Lockhart. .   Witmark: MPHC
BABBITT   Composition for 4 Insts.   4 W.W. . . . . . . . .   NME XXII#4(1949)
BACH, J.S.   Prelude, Fugue; #14 from W. T. C.
      Arr: Fl, Ob, Cl, Bn(BsCl) by Kessler. . . .   Rubank
CARTER   Eight Etudes and a Fantasia (1950).   4 W.W. . . . . . . . . . . .
DOMANSKY   Divertimento.   2Cl, Hn, Bn. . . . . . . . . . .   Schmidt(1936); Andraud
DURAND   Chaconne, Op 62.   Fl, Ob, Cl, Bn(BsCl). . . . . . .   Presser
DUREY   Quar.   4 Winds. . . . . . . . . . . . . . . . . . .
EGGE   Quar.   4 W.W. . . . . . . . . . . . . . . . . . . . .
FISCHER   17th-Cent. Banquet Music for 2Ob, 2Bn.
      Arr: WWQuar by Andraud. . . . . . . .   Andraud
FLEGIER   Quar--g mi.   2Ob, 2Bn. . . . . . . . . . .   Enoch(1906); Andraud
HAYDN   Divertimento--Bb.   Ed: 2Cl, 2Hn by Reichenbach. . .   Hansen(1932)
    Minuet de Boeuf.   Arr: 2Fl(Cl), 2Cl by Painter. . . . .   Remick; MPHC
IBERT   Quar, 2 mvts.   2Fl, Cl, Bn. . . . . . . . . .   Leduc(1923); MBaron
JONGEN   2 Paraphrases on Walloon Xmas Carols.
      Arr: 3Fl, AltFl(Cl, EH, Hn). . . . . . . . .   Andraud
KAUDER   Quar.   4 W.W.   . . . . . . . . . . . . . . .   NME XXII#3(1949)
KOLLESCHOWSKY   Adagio religioso.   2Cl, 2Bn. . . . . . .   Hoffman(Prague, 1846)
LANGE, G. FR.   Pastoral Quar.   2Ob, EH(Cl), Bn. . . . . . .   Seeling(1880); Andraud
LONG   In the Aquarium.   Fl, Ob(Fl), 2Cl.   . . . . . . . . .   CFisch
MIRANDOLLE   Quar--D.   4 W.W. . . . . . . . . .   Author publ.(Gravenhage, 1942)
MOZART   Advante (1791).   Arr: 2Fl, 2Cl by Leeuwen. . . . .   Spratt
PAGANINI   La Chasse.   Arr: Fl, Ob, Cl, Bn(BsCl) by Vognar. . .   Remick; MPHC
PALESTRINA   8 Ricercari in 4 Pts.   Ed: 4 winds by Fellerer. .   Schott(1933); AMP
PISK   Little Woodwind Music.   Ob, 2Cl, Bn. . . . . . . .   AMP
SCHWEGLER   Quar--Eb, Op3#2.   2Fl, 2Hn.   Ed: Schultz, in
            Erbe dt. Musik. . . . . . .   Nagel
SHAW   For the Gentlemen(publ. 1807).   Fl, 2Cl, Bn. . . . . . .   Merc
SPOHR   Conerto #1.   Arr: 2Cl, Cl(AltCl), Bn(BsCl) by Tallmadge. .   Remick; MPHC
STARK   Serenade--Eb, Op 55.   2Cl, BassetHn(Bn), BsCl(Bn). . .   C. F. Schmidt(1922)
WEIS-OSTBORN   Epilogue, Op 7.   2Hn, 2Bn. . . . . . . . . .   Ries & Erler(1900)

# FIVE INSTRUMENTS

### 5 INSTS. : including 1 Wind

Fl, StrQuar  unless otherwise given.

BEACH   Th. & Var. , Op 80 (1916). . . . . . . . . . . GSch(1920)
BERBIGUIER   Quint. . . . . . . . . . . . . . . . . . .
BOCCHERINI   18 Quints for Fl(Ob), StrQuar:
             6 Quint--D, C, d, Bb, G, Eb; Op 21
             6 Quint--Eb, g, C, D, Bb, D; Op 25
             6 Quint        ; Op 45 . . . . . . . . . . . .
BORDES   Suite Basque--D, Op 6. . . . . . . . . . . . Bornemann(Paris,1901); B-N
BOURGAULT-DUCOUDRAY   Abergavenny. . . . . . . . . Lemoine
BRANDTS BUYS   Quint--D. . . . . . . . . . . . . . . Doblinger(1903); B-N
FÜRSTENAU   Quint, Op 28. . . . . . . . . . . . . . . Simrock
GABRIELSKI   Quint, Op 103. . . . . . . . . . . . . . Kistner
GINASTERA   Impressions of Puna. . . . . . . . . . . Edit. Coop. ; SMPC
HARRIS   4 Minutes & 20 Seconds (1934). . . . . . . . GSch(1935)
HAYDN   Quintours #1, 4, 7, 8, 12. [Arr. ?] . . . . . . . . Andraud
KROMMER   Quints--D, e, C, Eb, d, G, Eb, G; Op 49, 55, 58, 66, 92,
                 101#6, 104#7, 109#8. . . . . . . .
KUHLAU   3 Quints--D, e mi, A; Op 51.  Fl, Vl, 2Va, Vc. . . . . Simrock
KUMMER   Quint--D, Op 66.  Fl, Vl, 2Va, Vc. . . . . . . . B&H
LANGE, HANS   Quint--C; Op 43. . . . . . . . . . . . Author publ.(Berlin, 1941)
MOLIQUE.  Quint--D, Op 35 (1848).  Fl, Vl, 2Va, Vc. . . . . Rudall(1883)
PISTON   Quint (1942). . . . . . . . . . . . . . . . . Arrow
POPP   Serenade de Concert, Op 333. . . . . . . . . . B-N
PORTER   Quintet in One Movement. . . . . . . . . . . Publ. in "Musicology"
PURCELL   Suite.  Ed: M. Holmes, from BrMus MS. . . . . McG & M, ECSch
REICHA   Quint--A, Op 105. . . . . . . . . . . . . . . B&H
RIES   Quint--b mi; Op 107 (1818).  Fl, Vl, 2Va, Vc. . . . . Peters, B&H
ROMBERG, A.J.   8 Quints, Op 41.  Fl, Vl, 2Va, Vc. . . . . Schott
ROMBERG, A.J. & BERNH.   3 Quints--D, C, G; Op 1.
                 Fl, Vl, 2Va, Vc. . . . . B&H
STÖHR   Suite--e mi, Op 52. . . . . . . . . . . . . . E. Strache(Vienna, 1922)
STRINGFIELD   Prelude & Fugue (1924). . . . . . . . . . . . . .
           Indian Sketches (1924). . . . . . . . . . . . .
THIEME   Serenade.  Fl, 3Vl, Vc. . . . . . . . . . . . Kallmeyer(1938)
TOESCHI   Quint--F, Op 3#6.  Ed: Fl, Vl, Va, Vc, Cb by Riemann. B&H(1914)
TOVEY   Var. on a Theme of Gluck--g mi, Op 28. . . . . . . Schott(London, 1914)
TUTHILL   Nocturne, Op 4 (1933). . . . . . . . . . . . Privately printed
VAN VACTOR   Quint (1932). . . . . . . . . . . . . . SPAM(1941); GSch
WALCKIERS   Quint--a mi, Op 90. . . . . . . . . . . . Costallat(c1855)


Ob, StrQuar

BAX   Quint--g mi (1923). . . . . . . . . . . . . . . OUP(1925); B-N
BLISS   Quint. . . . . . . . . . . . . . . . . . . . . OUP(1927); Andraud
BOCCHERINI   See under Fl, StrQuar category.
CADOW   Var. on a Swedish Folksong. . . . . . . . . . Grosch(1939)
CRUSELL   Divertimento, Op 9. . . . . . . . . . . . . Peters
FINZI   Interlude. . . . . . . . . . . . . . . . . . . B&H(1936); B-N

<u>Ob, StrQuar</u> cont.


KAUN, B.   Quint.   . . . . . . . . . . . . . . . .   Andraud
McBRIDE   Oboe Quintet (1937).  . . . . . . . . . . . . .   GSch
REICHA   Quint.   [Op 107?].   . . . . . . . . . . . .   MBaron


<u>Cl, StrQuar</u>  unless otherwise given.


AMES   Quint.   . . . . . . . . . . . . . . . . . . . .
BALORRE   Quint--g mi.  . . . . . . . . . .   Hamelle(1906)
BEN-HAIM   Quint.   [Cl, StrQuar?].  . . . . . . . . . . .
BLATT   Th. & Var.   Cl in Bb. . . . . . . . . . . . .   Simrock
BLISS   Quint.   Cl in A. . . . . . . . .   Novello(1933); Andraud
BRAHMS   Quint--b mi, Op 115.   Cl in A.   . . . . . .   Simrock(1892); several
COLERIDGE-TAYLOR   Quint--A, Op 10.   Cl in A.  . . . . .   B&H(1906); AMP
FUCHS, R.   Quint, Op 102.   Cl in A. . . . . . . . . .   Robitschek(1919)
GARDNER   Quint.   . . . . . . . . . . . . . . . .
HILL, EDW. B.   Quint (1945).   Cl in A. . . . . . .
HINDEMITH   Quint, Op 30.  . . . . . . . . . . . . .
HOESSLIN   Quint--c# mi.   Cl in A.   . . . . . . . .   Simrock(1924); AMP
HOLBROOKE   Cavatina & Var. --d mi, Op 27#1.   Cl in Bb.  . .   Chester(1914); Andraud
            Quint--G, Op 27#2.   . . . . . . . . . .   Goodwin & Tabb(1914)
HOWELLS   Rhapsodic Quintet, Op 31.   Cl in A.  . . . . . .   Stainer & B(1920); Andraud
JACOB   Quint.   Cl in Bb. . . . . . . . . .   Novello(1946)
KORNAUTH   Quint, Op 33. . . . . . . . . . . . . .   Doblinger; AMP
KREHL   Quint--A, Op 19.   Cl in A. . . . . . . . . .   Simrock(1902); AMP
KREIN   2 Suites, Esquisses hebraiques; Op 12, 13(c1910).  . . .   Jurgenson(c1913); Andraud
KREUTZER, ROD.   Quint--C.   Cl(Ob), StrQuar. . . . . . .   Costallat
KROMMER   Quint--Bb, Op 95.   Cl, Vl, 2Va, Vc. . . . . . .
LEDERER   Quint--Bb, Op 45.   . . . . . . . . . .   Grosch(1941)
LUENING   Quint, Op 4 (1920).   StrQuar, Cl oblig.  . . . . . .
MARTEAU, H.   Quint--C, Op 13.   Cl in A.  . . . . . . . .   Alsbach(1909); Andraud
MOORE   Quint (1946). . . . . . . . . . . . .   Ozalid prints available from comp.
MOZART   Quint--A, K 581 (1789).   Cl in A. . . . . . . .   Heckel(1852), B&H; several
MÜLLER, S. W.   Divertimento--a mi, Op 13.   Cl in A. . . . .   B&H(1927-28); Andraud
PAPE   Adagio.  . . . . . . . . .   Cranz(1863)
PORTER   Quint (1929).   Cl in Bb. . . . . . . . . . .
RAPHAEL   Serenade--F, Op 4.   Cl in Bb.  . . . . . . .   Simrock(1926); AMP
REGER   Quint--A, Op 146.   Cl in A.   . . . . . . . .   Peters(1916); AMP
REICHA   Quint--Bb, Op 89.   Cl, StrQuar(Vl, 2Va, Vc).  . . . .   B&H
         Quint--f mi, Op 107.   Cl(Ob), StrQuar.  . . . . . . . . . .
RIDKY   Quint--A, Op 5.  . . . . . . . . . .   Sadlo(1926), not yet printed
ROMBERG, A. J.   Quint, Op 57.   Cl, Vl, 2Va, Vc. . . . . . .   Peters, Simrock
SCHUBERT, KURT   Quint--d mi. . . . . . . . . . .   Verlagsanst. dt. Tonkunstler(1925)
SOMERVELL   Quint (1919) . . . . . . . . . . . . . . . . .
SPOHR   2 Sets of Var., Op 34, 81.   Cl in Bb.  . . . . . .   C. F. Schmidt
STIEBER   Quint--A.   . . . . . . . . . . . . . . .   Gebauer(1920)
STRANG   Quint (1933).   . . . . . . . . . . . . . . . . .
STRÄSSER   Quint--G, Op 34.   Cl in A.   . . . . . . . .   Simrock(1920); AMP
TÄGLICHSBECK   Quint--Bb, Op 44. . . . . . . .   Heinrichshofen(1863)
TUTHILL   Quint (1936).  . . . . . . . . . . . . .   Ozalid prints available.
WALTHEW   Quint.   . . . . . . . . . . . . . . . . . . . .
WEBER, C. M.   Quint--Bb, Op 34 (1815).   Cl in Bb.  . . . . .   Costallat(1850); MBaron
WEISSE   Quint (1928). . . . . . . . . . . . . . .

Hn, StrQuar  unless otherwise given.

DAUPRAT   3 Quints--F, E, Eb; Op 6. . . . . . . . . . .  Lemoine
KREUZ   Quint--Eb, Op 49. . . . . . . . . . . . . . .  Augener(1901)
MOZART   Quint--Eb, K 407 (1783).  Hn, Vl, Va, 2Vc(or Vl, 2Va, Vc). . Peters(1854); B&H
REICHA   Quint--E, Op 106. . . . . . . . . . . . . . .  B&H
SINIGAGLIA   Quint. . . . . . . . . . . . . . . . . . . .
STRONG   Quint. . . . . . . . . . . . . . . . . . . . .


Misc:  1 Wind, StrQuar

DUNCAN, J. Divertimento. Tb StrQuar. . . . . . . . . .  Ms available from comp.,
                                                        Montgomery T. C., Ala.
GOEB   Quint.  Tb, StrQuar. . . . . . . . . . . . . .  Ms available from comp., Juilliard
LANGE, HANS   Quint--e mi, Op 13.  Bn, StrQuar. . . . . .  Author Publ. (Berlin, 1937)
REICHA   Quint.  Bn, StrQuar. . . . . . . . . . . . . . . . . . . .


## 5 INSTS. : including 1 Wind & Pf(Keyboard, etc.)

Fl, Vl, Va, Vc, Hp

BECLARD d'HARCOURT   En regardant Watteau. . . . . . . .  Salabert(1942)
CRAS   Quint--A. . . . . . . . . . . . . . . . . . . .  Senart(1930); Andraud
DAMASE   Quint. . . . . . . . . . . . . . . . . . . ..  Lemoine; E-V, MBaron
FRANCAIX   Quint. . . . . . . . . . . . . . . . . . . .  Andraud
d'INDY   Suite en parties--A, Op 91 (1927).  Fl is oblig. . . . .  Heugel(1950); B-N
JONGEN   Concert a 5, Op 71. . . . . . . . . . . . . . .  Andraud
LANGE, HANS   Quint--A, Op 42. . . . . . . . . . . . . .  Author publ. (Berlin, 1938)
MALIPIERO   Sonata a 5. . . . . . . . . . . . . . . . .  Ricordi(1937); Andraud
PIERNE, GABR.   Var. libres et final, Op 51. . . . . . . . .  Salabert(1933); Andraud
PIERNE, PAUL   Var. au clair de lune. . . . . . . . . .  Lemoine(1935); Andraud
PILLOIS   Lyric Japanese Epigrams. . . . . . . . . . . .  Durand(1926); E-V
ROPARTZ   Prelude, Marine, & Songs. . . . . . . . . . .  Durand(1928); E-V
ROUSSEL   Serenade, Op 30 (1925). . . . . . . . . . . .  Durand(1926); E-V
SCHMITT   Suite en Rocaille (1935). . . . . . . . . . .  Durand(1935); E-V
SPELMAN   Le Pavillon sur l'Eau (1925). . . . . . . . .  Chester(1926); MBaron
TOURNIER   Suite.  . . . . . . . . . . . . . . . . . .  Lemoine(1929); Andraud


Fl, Vl, Va, Vc, Pf

BERTINI   Quint, after Nonet Op 107--D. . . . . . . . . .  Lemoine
CASTELBARCO   Quint--A, Op 42. . . . . . . . . . . . . .  Schott(1847)
CRAS   Quint--A.  Hp or Pf.  . . . . . . . . . . . . . .  Senart(1930); Andraud
HANSCHKE   Var. on a Children's Song. . . . . . . . . . .  Schott; AMP
HAYDN   Quar--G, Op 5#4.  Vc is ad lib.   Ed: Upmeyer. . . .  Nagel(1937); Andraud
JANITSCH   Sonata, Op 8.   Fl, Ob(Fl, Vl), Va(Gamba), Vc(Cb), Pf.
                          Ed: Wolff. . . . . . . . . . .  B&H(1937)
SANDBY   Quint--g mi.  . . . . . . . . . . . . . . . .  Skandinavisk(1937)
SPOHR   Quint, after Nonet--F, Op 31.  Ed: Schwencke. . . . . . . . . . . . . . . ?
STEVENS   Quint (1945). . . . . . . . . . . . . . . . .  SPAM(1948); GSch

## Misc: Fl, 3 Str. Pf(Hpschd)

CORETTE   5th Concerto.  Fl, 2Vl, Vc, Pf.  Ed: ? . . . . . . .  MBaron
DIAMOND   Quint--b mi (1937).  Fl, StrTrio, Pf.  . . . . . . . .  SPAM(1942); GSch
GABRIELI   Sonata.  3Fl(Vl), Pf, Vc ad lib.  Ed:  ? . . . . . .  Peters
HANDEL   Concerto #1--d mi.   Fl, Vl, Vc obl, Pf, Vc ad lib.
                    Ed: Zobeley. . . . . . . . .  Schott(1935); AMP
HANSCHKE   Var. on a Children's Song.  Fl, Vl, Va(Vl), Vc, Pf  ad lib. . Schott; AMP
JANITSCH   Sonata, Op 8.  Fl, Ob(Vl, Fl), Va(Gamba), Vc(Cb), Pf.
                    Ed: Wolff. . . . . . . . . .  B&H(1937)
SCARLATTI, A.   Sonate--F.  Fl, 2Vl, Pf, Vc ad lib.  Ed: Woehl.  Peters
SCHEIBE   Concerto for Fl--Bb.  Fl solo, 2Vl, Vc, Hpschd(Pf).  .  AMP
TELEMANN   Concerto di Camera.  Fl(Ob), 2Vl, Pf, Vc ad lib.  .
                    Ed: Friedrich. . . . . . . .  Schott(1939)

## Ob, 3 Str, Pf(Hp)

BEETHOVEN   Quint--Eb, Op 16 (c1797).  Ob, Vl, Va, Vc, Pf. * .  B&H; AMP
DUBOIS   Quint--F.  Vl, Ob(Cl), Va, Vc, Pf. . . . . . . . . .  Heugel(1905)
HANDEL   Concerto #2a from 3 Ob Concerti--Bb.
                Ob solo, 2Vl, Continuo(Pf&Vc).  In Werke XXI. .  B&H(1858)
MENDELSSOHN, J.   Quint.  Ob, Vl, Va, Vc, Pf. . . . . . . .  Eschig(1939)
ROSLAVETZ   Nocturne (1913).  Ob, 2Va, Vc, Hp. . . . . . . .  UE(1929)
TELEMANN   Concerto di Camera.  See Fl, 3Str, Pf category.

## Cl, Vl, Va, Vc, Pf  unless otherwise given.

DUBOIS   Quint--F.   See Ob, 3Str, Pf.
FIBICH   Quint--D, Op 42 (1894).   Vl, Cl, Hn(Va), Vc, Pf. . . . .  Urbanek(1896); Andraud
FRUGATTA   Quint. . . . . . . . . . . . . . . . . . . . . . . . . .
HAUER   Quint, Op 26.  . . . . . . . . . . . . . . . .  Schlesinger(1924)
KAHN   Quint--c mi, Op 54.  Cl, Vl, Hn(Va), Vc, Pf. . . . . . .  Bote & Bock(1910)
KALKBRENNER   Quint--a mi, Op 81.  Cl, Hn(Va), Vc, Cb, Pf.  .  B&H
LABOR   Quint--D, Op 11. . . . . . . . . . . . . . .  UE(1912)
WEINGARTNER   Quint--g mi, Op 50. . . . . . . . . . . .  B&H(1911); AMP

## Hn, Vl, Va, Vc, Pf

ALEXANDER FRIEDRICH   Quint--C, Op 25. . . . . . . . .  B&H(1939)
DRAESEKE   Quint--Bb, Op 48. . .. . . . . . . . . . . .  Kistner(1889)
VAUGHAN WILLIAMS   Quint (1905). . . . . . . . . . . . . . .

## Misc: including 1 Wind & Pf

SCHUMANN, ROBT.   Andante & Var.--Bb, Op 46 (1843).  Hn, 2Vc, 2Pf.  . . . . B&H
SPITZMÜLLER-HARMERSBACH   Divertimento, Op 6.  2Vl, Va, Bn, Pf.  . . . . UE(1933)
WIDOR   Serenade--Bb, Op 10.  Fl, Vl, Vc, Harmonium, Pf. . . . . . . . . . . Hamelle

*Both this and the Ob, Cl, Hn, Bn, Pf versions are authentic.

## 2 Winds, Vl, Va, Vc

BENTZON   Variazioni Interotti, Op 12.  With Cl, Bn.  . . . . .   Hansen(1928); Andraud
BLISS   Conversations (1920).  With Fl&BsFl, Ob&EH. . . . . .   UE, Curwen(1922-24)
BUTTING   Quint, Op 22.  With Ob, Cl. . . . . . . . . . . .   Tischer & J(1926)
ERLEBACH   Rhapsody Quint, Op 17 (1921).  Fl, EH(Ob). . . . .   Stainer & Bell(1927)
HIRSCHBACH   2 Quints--Bb, Eb; Op 41, 48.  Cl, Hn. . . . . . .   Siegel(1856-59)
KAMINSKI   Quint--f# mi.  Cl, Hn.  . . . . . . . . . . .   UE(c1930?)
MASSON   Quint.  Ob, Bn.  . . . . . . . . . . . . . .   Selva(Paris)
RUBBRA   The Buddha, Op 64.  Fl, Ob.  . . . . . . . . . .   Lengnick; Mills
SIERING   Serenade--G, Op 15.  Fl, Ob(Cl).  . . . . . . . . .   Hoffarth(1860)
TARP   Serenade.  Fl, Cl.  . . . . . . . . . . . . .   Kistner(1934); McG & M
TOCCHI   Arlecchino.  Fl, Cl.  . . . . . . . . . . . .   Carisch(1938)
VIDAL   Xmas Prelude.  Fl, Ob.  . . . . . . . . . . . .   Andraud
WHITE   4 Proverbs.  Fl, Ob.  . . . . . . . . . . . . .   Stainer & Bell(c1930)

## Misc:  including 2 Winds

HANDEL   Marches.   2Tt, 2Vl(Cl & Ob), Vc(any Bs inst. ).  . . .   Merc
HINDEMITH Tafelmusik, from "Plöner Musiktag. "
                              Fl, Tt(Cl), 2Vl, Vc.  . . . . .   Schott(1932); AMP
LOURIE   Pastoral de la Volga.  Ob, Bn, 2Va, Vc. . . . . . .   Eschig(1931-32); AMP
PLEYEL   3 Quints, Op 10.  Fl, Vl, Ob, Va, Bs[Cb?].  . . . .   Haviesen(Frankf't a/M)
PROKOVIEV   Quint, Op 39.  Ob, Cl, Vl, Va, Cb.  . . . . . .   Gutheil(1927); IMC
SEKLES   15 Little Chamber Pcs.  Fl, Cl, Va, Vc, Perc.  . . . . .
SLAVENSKI   In the Village, Op 6.  Fl, Cl, Vl, Va, Cb.  . . . .   Schott(1926); AMP
SOATTA   Quint.  Fl, 2Va, Bn, Vc.  . . . . . . . . . .   Ricordi
STICH   Quint.  Hn, Fl, Strs.  . . . . . . . . . . . . .
WEINGARTNER   Quint--C, Op 40.  2Vl, 2Ob, Vc.  . . . . . . .   B&H

## 5 INSTS. :  including 2 Winds & Pf(Keyboard, etc. )

## 2 Winds, Vl, Vc, Pf(Hp)

BACH, J. C.   Quint--D.  With Fl, Ob.  . . . . . . . . . .   McG & M
BAUSSNERN   Quint--F.  With Cl, Hn.  . .. . . . . . . . .   Simrock(1905); AMP
DUNHILL   Quint--Eb, Op 3 (1898).  Cl, Hn.  . . . . . . . .   Rudall Carte(1913)
FASCH   Sonate a 4--Bb.  Fl, Ob.  Ed: Dancker-Langer. . . . .   Nagel(1939); McG & M
FIBICH   Quint--D, Op 42 (1894).  Cl, Hn(Va).  . . . . . . .   Urbanek(1896); Andraud
HAYDN   Symph. Concertante, Op 84.  Ob, Bn.  Ed: Sitt. . . . .   B&H; AMP, IMC
KAHN   Quint--c mi, Op 54.  Cl(Vl), Hn(Va).  . . . . . . .   Bote & Bock(1910)
LACOMBE, L. B.   Quint--f# mi, Op 26.  Ob, Bn.  . . . . . .   Costallat
LEIDESDORF   Quint--Eb, Op 66.  Cl, Bn. . . . . . . . . .
LUTZ   Fantaisie Japon.  With 2Fl, uses Hp. . . . . . . . .   Paxton(c1920)
TELEMANN   Quar--G.  Fl, Ob.  Ed: Woehl. . . . . . . .   Rieter-B(1939); Peters

## 2 Winds, Va, Vc, Pf(Hp)

DELANNOY   Rapsodie.  With Tt, Sx.  . . . . . . . . . . .   Heugel(1934); Merc
JANITSCH   Sonata, Op 8.  With Fl, Ob(Fl).  Ed: Wolff. . . . .   B&H(1937)

2 Winds, Va, Vc, Pf(Hp) cont.

LIEBERSON   Quint (1934).   Ob, Bn. . . . . . . . . . . . . . . .
MOZART   Adagio & Rondo--c mi-maj, K 617 (1791).
                    Fl, Ob, Va, Vc, GlassHarmonica(Pf). . . . . .B&H(1883); AMP
ROTA   Quint.   Fl, Ob; uses Hp. . . . . . . . . . . . . Ricordi(1937)


Misc: including 2 Winds & Pf(etc.)

BEDFORD   Pathways of the Moon, Op 50.   Fl, Ob, Vl, Va, Pf. . Goodwin & Tabb
HINDEMITH   3 Pcs. for 5 Insts. (1932).   Cl, Tt, Vl, Cb, Pf. . . Schott(1934); Andraud
HUMMEL   2 Serenades, Op 63, 66.   Vl, Cl, Bn, Guitar, Pf. . . . . . . . . . .
KALKBRENNER   Quint--a mi, Op 81.   Cl, Hn, Vc, Cb, Pf. . . . B&H
ROUSSEAU   Bergers et Mages--Bb. (For Ob, Vl, Cb, Hp, Organ).
                    Arr: Ob, Bn, Vl, Vc, Pf. . Merc
VILLERS   Quint.   Ob, Hn, Cb, Pf, Hp. . . . . . . . . . . . Chatot(Paris, 1863)


### 5 INSTS.: including 3 Winds

CASELLA   Serenata--C.   Cl, Bn, Tt, Vl, Vc. . . . . . . . . . UE(1929); Andraud
HAYDN, MICH.   Divertimento--G.   Ed: Fl, Vl, Va, Hn, Bn by Perger. . B&H
NIELSEN, C. A.   Serenata Invano.   Cl, Bn, Hn, Vc, Cb. . . . . . McG & M
PALMER,   Concerto.   Fl, Vl, Cl, EH, Vc. . . . . . . . . . in Blueprint
SCARLATTI, D.   Sonate--D.   Ob, Cl, Bn, Vl, Vc.   Ed: ? . . . . B-N


### 5 INSTS.: including 3 Winds & Pf(Keyboard, etc.)

3 Winds, Vc, Pf

GABRIELI   Sonata.   With 3 Fl. . . . . . . . . . . . . . . Peters
SCARLATTI, A.   Quartetino.   With 3Fl.   Ed: Woehl. . . . . . Peters, MBaron
TANSMAN   Divertimento (1943).   With Ob, Cl, Tt. . . . . . . AMP
TELEMANN   Quatuor--d mi.   With 3Fl.   Ed: Seiffert, in D. d. T. B&H(192?)


Misc: including 3 Winds & Pf(Hp)

MORTARI   Concertino (1925-37).   Vl, Cl, Tt, Bn, Pf. . . . . . . . . . . . .
ROCCA   Storiella.   Bn, 2Tt, Pf, Hp. . . . . . . . . . . . . Ricordi(1937)
RUYNEMAN   Divertimento.   Fl, Cl, Hn, Va, Pf. . . . . . . . Chester(1928); Andraud
SAUGUET   Pres du bal.   Fl, Cl, Bn, [Va?], Pf. . . . . . . . Rouart(1929)
                    Divertissement.   Fl, Cl, Va, Bn, Pf. . . . . . . . Eschig(1934); Andraud


### 5 INSTS.: including 4 Winds

HANDEL   Marches.   2Tt, 2Vl(Cl&Ob), Vc(any Bs inst.).   . . . Merc
                    2 Marches.   2Tt, 2Ob(Cl), Vc(Bn).   . . . . . . . . MBaron

Misc. cont.

PRÄGER, H. A.   Quint--Bb, Op 12.  Fl, 2Cl, Va, Bn.  . . . . .  B&H
SCHWARTZ, (L?)  Oriental Suite.  WWQuar, Perc.  . . . . .  UE(1932); Andraud
SEIFF  6 Bavarian Fanfares (1820).  4Tt, Tymp. . . . . . .  McG & M
STRAVINSKY  Pastorale.  Vl(Sop. Voice), Ob, EH, Cl, Bn.  . . .  Schott(1934; AMP
STRECK  8 Franconian Fanfares (1940).  4Tt, Tymp. .  . . .  McG & M
THOMSON  Sonata da Chiesa (1926).  Eb Cl, Tt, Va, Hn, Tb.  . .  NME XVIII#1(1944)
WASSILENKO  On Turkish Folk Songs, Op 65.  WWQuar, Perc..  UE(1932); Peters

## 5 INSTS. :  including 4 Mixed Woodwinds & Pf(Keyboard, etc. )

### Fl, Ob, Cl, Bn, Pf(Hp

CAPLET  Quint (1898). . . . . . . . . . . . . . . .  . . . . . . .
CETTIER  Quint--G. . . . . . . . . . . . . . . . .  Senart(1927)
DUKELSKY  Hymn, Waltz, Paso Doble (1940). . . . . . . .  CFisch(1946)
GHEDINI  Concerto. . . . . . . . . . . . . . . . . .  Ricordi(1937); Andraud
IPPOLITOV-IVANOV  An Evening in Georgia, Op 69a.  Hp or Pf.  . . UE(1926); Peters
LONGO  Pastoral Scene. . . . . . . . . . . . . . .  Curci(1926); Andraud
MAGNARD  Quint--d mi, Op 8 (1894). . . . . . . . .  Rouart(1904); Andraud

### Fl, Cl, Bn, Hn, Pf

ABRAMSKY  Concertino. . . . . . . . . . . . . .  UE(1929); Andraud
BLANC  Quint, Op 37. . . . . . . . . . . . . . .  Costallat
DUNCAN  Quint, Op 38. . . . . . . . . . . . . . .  Rudall Carte(c1920)
HUBER  Quint, Op 136. . . . . . . . . . . . . . .  Hug(1920); Andraud
RIMSKY-KORSAKOV  Quint--Bb (1876). . . . . . . .  Belaiev(1910); Andraud
RUBINSTEIN  Quint--F, Op 55. . . . . . . . . . .  Hamelle(1861); Andraud
SPOHR  Quint--c mi, Op 52. . . . . . . . . . . .  Peters; McG & M new ed.
TAUBERT  Quint--Bb, Op 48. . . . . . . . . . . .  Bote & Bock(1892); Andraud

### Ob, Cl, Bn, Hn, Pf

BEETHOVEN  Quint--Eb, Op 16 (c1797). . . . . . . . . .  B&H; AMP, IMC
GIESEKING  Quint--Bb. . . . . . . . . . . . . . .  Oertel(1923); Andraud
HERZOGENBERG  Quint--Eb, Op 43. . . . . . . . . .  Peters(1888)
HÜTTEL  Divertimento Grotesque. . . . . . . . . .  Libr. of Congress(1929)
MOZART  Sinfonia Concertante--Eb, K 297b (1778). * . . . . . .  C-B
        Quint--Eb, K 452 (1784). . . . . . . . .  Andre(1855); AMP, MBaron
PAUER  Quint--F, Op 44. . . . . . . . . . . . . .  Schott(1856)
RICE  Quint--Bb, Op 2. . . . . . . . . . . . . .  Simrock(1898); Andraud
SPINDLER  Quint, [Op 2?]. . . . . . . . . . . . .  . . . . . . Andraud
        Quint--F, Op 360. . . . . . . . . . . . .  Leuckart(1888)
STEPHEN  Quint--d mi, Op 3. . . . . . . . . . . .  B&H(London, 1899)
THIERIOT  Quint--a mi, Op 80. . . . . . . . . . .  Simrock(1903); Andraud
VERHEY  Quint--Eb, Op 20. . . . . . . . . . . . .  B&H(1884); Andraud
VOLBACH  Quint--Eb, Op 24. . . . . . . . . . . .  B&H(1902); AMP

*Mozart's original scoring of this for Fl, Ob, Hn, Bn was lost.

## 2 Ct, Tb, Bar, Organ

BACH, J. S.   In dulci jubilo.   Arr: King. . . . . . . . . . . . . . . . . Mus f Brass
            Jesu, nun sei gepreistet, from Cantata 41.  Arr: King. . . . . Mus f Brass
BONELLI   Toccata.   Ed: King. . . . . . . . . . . . . . . . . . . . Mus f Brass
BRAHMS   O Welt ich muss dich lassen.  Arr: King. . . . . . . . . . . Mus f Brass
GABRIELI   Sonata pian e forte.  Arr. . . . . . . . . . . . . . . . . Mus f Brass
KING   Prelude & Fugue. . . . . . . . . . . . . . . . . . . . . . . Mus f Brass
MARCELLO   Psalm #19 for Organ, 1st mvt.  Arr: King. . . . . . . . . Mus f Brass
REICHE   Sonata #7.  Arr: King. . . . . . . . . . . . . . . . . . . Mus f Brass

## Misc: 4 Mixed Brass & Pf

BERNSTEIN   Brass Music.   Tt, Hn, Tb, Tuba,  Pf.
                          Rondo for Lifey:  Tt, Pf
                          Elegy  for Mippy I:  Hn, Pf          available also
                          Elegy  for Mippy II:  Tb, alone      individually
                          Waltz for Mippy III: Tuba, Pf
                          Fanfare for Bima: Tt, Hn, Tb, Tuba. . . . GSch(1950)
SATTER   Quint--Eb, Op 6.  2Flugelhn(Cl), AltHn, Bar(Bn), Pf. . . .  Hoffarth(1868)
SPEER   Sonata--d mi.  4Tb, Pf.  Ed: Schultz, in Erbe dt. Musik. . . . Nagel(1941)

### 5  INSTS. : including 4 Misc. Winds & Pf

HARRIS   Quint (1932).   Fl, Ob, Hn, Bn, Pf. . . . . . . . . . . . . . . . . . .
KALMAN   Un Coin sous les Toits.  4Cl, Pf.  . . . . . . . . . Eschig; AMP, MBaron
KRIEGER   Partie--F.  2Ob, EH, Bn, Pf.  Ed: Seiffert. . . . . . Kistner(1925); Andraud
LOEFFLER   Ballade carnavalesque (1904).  Fl, Ob, Sx, Bn, Pf. . . . . . . . . . . .
McKAY   American Street Scenes(1936).  Cl, Tt, 2Sx, Pf. . . . . . . . . . . . . . .
PFEIFFER   Sonata--G.  Fl, Ob, Hn, Bn, Pf.  Ed: Lauschmann. . Hofmeister(1939); Andraud
PONCHIELLI   "Quartet. "   Fl, Ob, LittleClarino, Clarino, Pf.  . Ricordi
REICHARDT   Quint.  2Fl, 2Hn, Pf.  . . . . . . . . . . . . . . . . . . . . . . .
SATTER   Quint--Eb, Op 6.  See 4 Mixed Brass & Pf.
SCHMIKERER   Suites--F, d mi; Nr 1, 2.  4 Winds, Pf.  Ed: Woehl . . . Bärenreiter
TURECHEK   Fl Quint.  4Fl, Pf. . . . . . . . . . . . . . . . Witmark; MPHC
WOOLLETT   Cinq pieces.  2Fl, Cl, Hn, Pf. . . . . . . . . . . . . . . . . . . .

### 5  INSTS. :  5 Woodwinds

## 5 Mixed Cl

MOZART   Adagio--Bb, K 411 (1782).  2Cl, 3BassetHn. . . . . B&H(1883)
        ditto . . .  Arr: 3Cl, AltCl, BsCl by Goldman. . . . McG & M
WEBER, C. M.   Minuet from Cl Quint--Bb, Op 34 (1815).
              Arr: 3Cl, AltCl(Sx), BsCl(Bn).  . . . . C-B

**5 Sx**   cont.

HOLBROOKE   Serenade . . . . . . . . . . . . . . . . .
KROLL   4 Pcs. for 5 Saxes.   2AltSx, 2TenSx, BarSx. . . . . .   Thomas-Cole; AMP
LÖBL   Quint.  Sx Quintet.  ?   . . . . . . . . . . . . .   Author publ. (Vienna, 1941)


**Fl, Ob, 2Cl, Bn**

DAHLHOFF   Waldegeheimnisse. . . . . . . . . . . . . . .   Schmidt(Heilbronn, 1925)
FITELBERG   Quint.   Fl, Ob, Cl, BsCl, Tb(Bn). . . . . . . .   Balan(1931); MBaron
KREUTZER, (K. ?)   1st mvt. of Quar--Eb.  Arr: WWQuar, BsCl ad lib. . . .   Alfred
LABATE   Intermezzo; Scherzino. . . . . . . . . . . . .   Spratt
MORITZ, KURT   Heitere Suite, Op 12. . . . . . . . . . .   Ries & Erler(1938); Andraud


**WWQuint: Fl, Ob(EH), Cl, Bn, Hn**

_____   Collection of 21 WWQuints.  Ed: Andraud. . . . . .   Andraud
_____   Juilliard Series, 2 Bks.  Ed: Barrere. . . . . . .   GSch
_____   English Folk Song, Turtle Dove.  Arr: Hirsch. . . .   Leeds
_____   Short Quint--Bb, mvts. by 3 composers.  Ed: Pierce .   Remick: MPHC
AMBROSIUS   Quint--b mi, Op 57. . . . . . . . . . . . . .   Author publ. (Leipzig, 1925)
BACH, J. S.   Saraband from 1st French Suite.  Arr. . . . . . .   Boosey
             Prelude, Fugue #22 from W. T. C.  Arr: Kessler. .   Rubank
             Badinerie; Fugue--c mi.  Arr. . . . . . . . . .   Presser
             Bouree from Overture #3--D.  Arr:--F by Orem .   Presser(1940)
BAKALEINIKOFF   Intro. & Scherzo. . . . . . . . . . . . .   Belwin
BALAY   Petite Suite Miniature, 18th Cent. . . . . . . . .   Andraud
        Menuet & Rondo.  Ed: Waln. . . . . . . . . . . .   Kjos
BARRAINE   Ouvrage de Dame. . . . . . . . . . . . . . .   Andraud
BARROWS   March for WWQuint. . . . . . . . . . . . . .   GSch(1950)
BARTHE   Aubade. . . . . . . . . . . . . . . . . . . .   Pinatel; Andraud
         Passacaille. . . . . . . . . . . . . . . . . .   Leduc(1899); MBaron
BEACH   Pastorale. . . . . . . . . . . . . . . . . . .   CompPr
BEETHOVEN   Sextet--Eb, Op 71 (c1792).  Arr: Stark. . . . .   Sikorski(1895); Andraud
            Var. from StrQuar--A, Op 18 #5 (1801).  Arr.. . . . . . . . .   Andraud
            Minuet, Andante, Var.  Arr. . . . . . . . . . . . . . . . .   Andraud
BENTZON   Racconto #5. . . . . . . . . . . . . . . . .   McG & M
BEREZOWSKY   Suite #1, Op 11 (1928) . . . . . . . . . .   Russ. M-V(1930); Andraud
             Suite #2, Op 22 (1937) . . . . . . . . . . .   Mills
BEYTHIEN   Quint--F, Op 7. . . . . . . . . . . . . . . .   Author publ. (Dresden, 1925)
BLUMER   Suite, Serenade, & Th. with Var. --F, Op 34. . . . .   Simrock(1918); AMP
         Quint--Bb, Op 52. . . . . . . . . . . . . . . .   Zimmerman(1924); Andraud
         Tanzsuite--D, Op 53.. . . . . . . . . . . . . .   Simrock(1925); AMP
BORCH   Sunrise on the Mts.. . . . . . . . . . . . . . .   Belwin
BORKOVEC   Quint (1932). . . . . . . . . . . . . . . .   Hudebni Matice(1936); Andrau
BOROWSKY   Madrigal to the Moon. . . . . . . . . . . .   Boosey
BOZZA   Var. sur un theme libre, Op 42. . . . . . . . . .   Leduc; MBaron
        Andante & Scherzo, Op 48. . . . . . . . . . . .   Leduc; MBaron
BRESCIA   Dithyrambic Suite.. . . . . . . . . . . . . . . . . . .
          2nd Suite, (Rhapsodic).  [WWQuint?] . . . . . . . . . . .
BRICCIALDI   Quint--D, Op 124. . . . . . . . . . . . . .   Schott(1875)
BROD   1st Quint, Op 2. . . . . . . . . . . . . . . . .   Lemoine
       2nd Quint. . . . . . . . . . . . . . . . . . . .   Lemoine(1921)
CAILLET   Overture--Bb. . . . . . . . . . . . . . . . .   E-V
CARABELLA   Suite. . . . . . . . . . . . . . . . . . .   Ricordi(1933); Andraud

WWQuint  cont.

CHRETIEN   Quint.  . . . . . . . . . . . . . . . . . B-N, Andraud
CLAPP   Prelude & Finale. . . . . . . . . . . . . . Boosey
COHEN   Quint #2. . . . . . . . . . . . . . . . . . Belwin
COLOMER   Minuet & Bouree. . . . . . . . . . . . . C-B, Andraud
COWELL   Suite.  . . . . . . . . . . . . . . . . . . Merc, McG & M
DANZI   Quint--g mi, Op 56#2.  Ed: Riemann, in D. T. B. XXVII. . . B&H(1914); Andraud
           Quint--e mi, Op 67#2.  Ed: Schultz, in Erbe dt. Musik.  . . Nagel(1941)
           Gypsy Dance. Arr: Maganini. . . . . . . . . CFisch
DELIBES   Petite Marche.  Arr: Barrere. . . . . . . . Juilliard Ed; GSch
DESLANDRES   Quint.  . . . . . . . . . . . . . . . . B-N, Andraud
DESPORTES   Prelude, Var., Finale on a Gregorian Chant. . MBaron
DOUGLAS   Dance Caricatures. . . . . . . . . . . . . Peters
DUBOIS   1st Suite.  Arr. . . . . . . . . . . . . . . Merc
EGIDI   Quint--Bb, Op 18. . . . . . . . . . . . . . . Verl. f. mus. Kultur(1937)
EMBORG   Quint, Op 74. . . . . . . . . . . . . . . . Edit. Dania(1937)
ERDLEN   Little Var. on a Spring Song, Op 27#1. . . . . . Zimmerman(1932); Andraud
ESCHPAY   Marische Melody. . . . . . . . . . . . . . Andraud
ESSEX   Quint. . . . . . . . . . . . . . . . . . . . . Peters
FERNANDEZ   Suite for Wind Insts. --F. . . . . . . . . AMP; MBaron
FÖRSTER   Quint--D, Op 95 (1909). . . . . . . . . . . Hudebni Matice(1925); Andraud
FRAGALE   WWQuint. . . . . . . . . . . . . . . . . . AMP; MBaron
FÜSSL   Kleine Kammermusik. . . . . . . . . . . . . Bärenreiter(1943)
GERSTER   Heitere Musik. . . . . . . . . . . . . . . Schott(1938); Andraud
GOULD   Pavanne from Amer. Symphonette #2.  Arr: Taylor. Mills
GOUNOD   Funeral March of Marionette. Arr: Teague.  . . Broadcast; AMP
GRAINGER   Walking Tune. . . . . . . . . . . . . . . Schott(1912); Andraud
GRIMM, C. H.   A Little Serenade, Op 36.; Intrada: Hn
                           Alla Sarabanda: Cl, Bn
                           Scherzino: Fl, Ob
                           Finale: WWQuint . . . . . . . . . Andraud
GUENTHER, R.  Rondo. . . . . . . . . . . . . . . . . C-B
GUENTZEL   Tarentella.  . . . . . . . . . . . . . . . Barnhouse
GUILMANT   Canzonetta. Arr: Taylor. . . . . . . . . . Remick; MPHC
HAAS   Dechovy kvintet, Op 10 (1929). . . . . . . . . Sadlo(1935)
HAMERIK   WWQuint. . . . . . . . . . . . . . . . . . McG & M
HANDEL   6 Little Fugues.  Arr; Bauer. . . . . . . . . Broadcast; AMP
HAYDN   Largo from StrQuar, Op 76#5.  Arr. . . . . . . Presser
           From a Klavier Trio--C.  Arr: Muth. . . . . . . Hofmeister(1929); Andraud
           Menuet.  Arr. . . . . . . . . . . . . . . . . Andraud
           Presto.  Arr. . . . . . . . . . . . . . . . . Andraud
           Divertimento.  Arr. . . . . . . . . . . . . . Boosey
HEIDEN   Sinfonia. . . . . . . . . . . . . . . . . . . Spratt
HEIM   Quint--Eb. . . . . . . . . . . . . . . . . . . Schmidt(1903)
HERMANN   Collection of Str Ens. music. Bk II.  Arr: WWQuint. . . . B&H(1899)
HILLMAN   Capriccio, Op 56. . . . . . . . . . . . . . Andre(1923); Belwin
HINDEMITH   Kleine Kammermusik, Op 24#2. . . . . . . Schott(1922); AMP
HÖFFDING   WWQuint, Op 35. . . . . . . . . . . . . . McG & M
HOLBROOKE   Miniature Suite, Op 33b. . . . . . . . . Rudall Carte; Andraud
HOSMER   Fugue--C. . . . . . . . . . . . . . . . . . Gamble
HOYER   Serenade--F, Op 29. . . . . . . . . . . . . . Simrock(1924); AMP
HUGUENIN   Gavotte-Musette. . . . . . . . . . . . . Andraud
                    Menuet-Bouree. . . . . . . . . . . Andraud
HUNTER   Danse Humoreske. . . . . . . . . . . . . . CFisch
IBERT   3 Short Pcs. (1921). . . . . . . . . . . . . . Leduc(1930); MBaron

WWQuint   cont.

| | |
|---|---|
| INGENHOVEN   Quint--C. . . . . . . . . . . . . . . | Wunderhorn(1912); Andraud |
| JACOBI   Scherzo (1936). . . . . . . . . . . | CFisch |
| JAMES   Suite, 4 mvts. (1936). . . . . . . . . . . | CFisch(1938) |
| JIRAK   Quint. . . . . . . . . . . . . . . . . . . . . . | |
| JONGEN   Preamble & Dances, Op 98. . . . . . . . . | Andraud |
| Concerto, Op 124. . . . . . . . . . . . . | MBaron |
| JUON   Quint--Bb, Op 84. . . . . . . . . . . . | Birnbach(1930); Andraud |
| KARREN   Little Tale from Brittany. . . . . . . . . . | Andraud |
| KAUFFMAN, FR.   Quint--Eb, Op 40. . . . . . . . . | Heinrichschofen(1905); Andraud |
| KEITH   Quint. . . . . . . . . . . . . . . . . | Boosey |
| KERN   Quint. . . . . . . . . . . . . . . . . | Grosch(1942) |
| KLUGHARDT   Quint--C, Op 79. . . . . . . . . . . . | Zimmerman(1901); Andraud |
| KUBIK   WWQuint (1937). . . . . . . . . . . . . | |
| KÜHNEL   Deutsche Ostseebilder. . . . . . . . . | Grosch(1942) |
| LABEY   Quint.  . . . . . . . . . . . . . . . . | Eschig(1923) |
| LANGE, HANS   Quint--D, Op 14. . . . . . . | Author publ. (Berlin, 1937) |
| Böhmische Musikanten--Ab, Op 40. . . . . | Author publ. (Berlin, 1937) |
| LAURISCHKUS   Lithuanian Suite, Op 23. . . . . . . . | Simrock(1914); Andraud |
| LECLAIR   Minuet & Hunting Scene. Arr. . . . . . . . | Andraud |
| LEFEBVRE   Prelude. Ed: Waln. . . . . . . . . . | Kjos |
| Suite, Op 57. . . . . . . . . . . . . | Hamelle(1910); C-B |
| LENDVAI   Quint--Ab, Op 23. . . . . . . . . . . . | Simrock(1922); AMP |
| LILGE   Var. &Fugue, Op 67. . . . . . . . . . . | Kistner(1937); Andraud |
| LINDNER   Quint--Bb, Op 1.  . . . . . . . . . . . . . | |
| LISZT   Pastoral, Longing for Home, Eclog; from "Annees" for Pf. Arr.  . . . Andraud | |
| LUENING   Fuguing Tune for Winds (1941). . . . . . . . | AMP |
| MANDIC   Quintet.  Uses Ob or EH. . . . . . . . . . | UE(1933) |
| MARTIN   Prestissimo. . . . . . . . . . . . . . . . | Boosey |
| MASON   Divertimento, Op 26b (1927). . . . . . . . . | Witmark(1936); MPHC |
| McBRIDE   Jam Session (1941). . . . . . . . . . . | CompPr |
| McCALL   2 Tunes from Mother Goose. . . . . . . . . | Andraud |
| McKAY   Quint (1932). . . . . . . . . . . . . . . . . | |
| Joyful Dance.  . . . . . . . . . . . . . . | Merc |
| MERECHAL, (H. ?) Night Watch Tune of King Rene. . . . . | Andraud |
| MERECHAL, H.   Air du Guet.  . . . . . . . . . . . | Merc |
| MILHAUD   Chimney of King Rene, 7 mvts.  Uses Fl & Picc.. | MBaron |
| Two Sketches: Madrigal, Pastorale. . . . . . . | Merc |
| MOORE   Quint (1942). . . . . . . . . . . . . . . . | SPAM(1947); GSch |
| MORITZ, EDV.   Quint, Op 41. . . . . . . . . . . . . | Zimmerman(1928); Andraud |
| MOUSSORGSKY   Chickens in Their Shells, from "Pictures.". Arr: Kessler . . . Rubank | |
| MOZART   Quar for Ob & Str--F, K 370. Arr: Cailliet. . . | E-V |
| Adagio for Cl & BassetHn--Bb, K 411. Arr: Weigelt. . . | Leuckart(1926) |
| Menuet. Ed: Waln. . . . . . . . . . . . . . | Kjos |
| Minuet. Arr. . . . . . . . . . . . . . . . | Andraud |
| German Dance. Arr. . . . . . . . . . . . . | Andraud |
| Divertimento #8--F, K 213. Arr: Weigelt. . . . | Leuckart(1928) |
| Divertimento #13--F, K 253. Arr: Weigelt. . . | Leuckart(1932) |
| Divertimento #14--Bb, K 270. Arr: Weigelt. . . | Leuckart(1928) |
| MÜLLER, P. 3 Quints--Eb, c mi, A.  . . . . . . . . | Ruhle(1874) |
| MÜLLER-RUDOLSTADT   Die Leineweber. . . . . . . . | Grosch(1933) |
| NIELSEN, C. A.   Quint--A, Op 43. . . . . . . . . . | Hansen(1927); McG & M |
| NORMAND   Quint--E. . . . . . . . . . . . . . . . | Vernede(Versailles, 1890); B-N |
| ONSLOW   Quint--F, Op 81. . . . . . . . . . . . . | Kistner(1852); Andraud |
| PERISSAS   Scotch Suite.  . . . . . . . . . . . . . . | Andraud |

WWQuint   cont.

PERSICHETTI   Pastoral Quint. . . . . . . . . . . . Black & White repro.
PESSARD   Aubade--D, Op 6. . . . . . . . . . . . Leduc(1880); MBaron
                  Prelude & Minuet. . . . . . . . . . . . .MBaron
PFEIFFER   3 Petite Pcs. de Concert. . . . . . . . . Andraud
                  Pastorale. . . . . . . . . . . . . . . Andraud
PIERCE   Allegro Piacevole & Scherzo. . . . . . . . . Remick; MPHC
                  Romance. . . . . . . . . . . . . . . . Pro-Art
PIERNE, GABR.   Pastorale, Op 14#1. . . . . . . . . C-B, Andraud
PIERNE, PAUL   Suite pittoresque. . . . . . . . . . . Buffet(1936)
PLEYEL   Rondo.   Arr: Geiger. . . . . . . . . . . Remick; MPHC
                  Op 48.   Arr: Harris. . . . . . . . . . C-B
POLDOWSKI   Suite Miniature. Arr: Barrere. . . . . . Galaxy
PORSCH   Suite Modique. . . . . . . . . . . . . . . Remick; MPHC
RAMEAU   Acante et Cephise, Airs de Ballet. Arr: Desormiere. . . . MBaron
RANDERSON   Quint. . . . . . . . . . . . . . . . . . . . .
RAPOPORT   Indian Legend. . . . . . . . . . . . . . AMP
RAVEL   Piece en Forme de Habanero. Arr: Kessler. . . . Leduc(1934); Andraud
                  Pavane pour une infante defunte. Arr: Intravaia. . E-V
REICHA   Quints Nr 1-6--e, Eb, G, d, Bb, F; Op 88 . . . . . Simrock, Schott
                  Quints Nr 7-12--C, a, D, g, A, c; Op 91. . . . . . Simrock
                  Quints Nr 13-18--C, f, F, D, b, G; Op 99. . . . . . Simrock
                  Quints Nr 19-24--F, c, Eb, e, a, Bb; Op 100. . . . Costallat
                  Quint #1--e mi, Op 88. . . . . . . . . Andraud
                  Quint #2--Eb, Op 88. Ed: Weigelt. . . . . . . Leuckart(1937)
                  Quint #11--A, Op 91. . . . . . . . . . . . AMP
                  Quint #13--C, Op 99. . . . . . . . . . . . AMP
                  Intro. & Allegro. . . . . . . . . . . . . Merc
REIZENSTEIN   Quint. . . . . . . . . . . . . . . . B&H(1937); Andraud
ROPARTZ   2 Pcs. . . . . . . . . . . . . . . . . Durand(1926); E-V
RORICH   Quint--e mi, Op 58. . . . . . . . . . . . Zimmerman(1921); Andraud
SACHSSE   Suite--C, Op 32. . . . . . . . . . . . Böhm(1935); Andraud
SCHAEFER   Quint. . . . . . . . . . . . . . . . . Pazdirek(c1940?)
SCHMID   Quint--Bb, Op 28. . . . . . . . . . . . Schott(1921); AMP
SCHMUTZ   Scherzo Poetique. . . . . . . . . . . . C-B
SCHONBERG   Quint, Op 26. . . . . . . . . . . . . UE(1925); Andraud
SENAILLE, (J. B. ?)   Rondo-Serioso. Arr: Taylor. . . . . Mills
SMETACEK   Aud dem Leben der Insekten. . . . . . . Edit. Continental(Prague, 1939)
SOBECK   Quint--F, Op 9. . . . . . . . . . . . . Bote & Bock(1879); Andraud
                  2 Quints--Eb, g mi; Op 11, 14. . . . . . . Bosworth(1891); Andraud
                  ditto . . .1st, 3rd, 4th mvts; Op 11. 1st, 4th mvts; Op 14. . . . Belwin
                  Quint--Bb, Op 23. . . . . . . . . . . . Lehne(1897); Andraud
SODERO   Morning Prayer; Valse Scherzo . . . . . . . . AMP
SOMIS   Adagio & Allegro from Sonata for Vl, FigBs--d. Arr: Hernried. . . CFisch(1947)
SOWERBY   Quint (1916). . . . . . . . . . . . . SPAM(1931); GSch
                  Pop Goes the Weasel (1927). . . . . . . . . Fitzsimmons(1927); Andraud
STAINER   Scherzo, Op 27. . . . . . . . . . . . . Rudall(1929); Andraud
STARK   Quint, Op 44. . . . . . . . . . . . . . .
STRINGFIELD   A Moonshiner Laughs. . . . . . . . . Andraud
STRUBE   Quint (1930). . . . . . . . . . . . . . .
TAFFANEL   Quint--g mi. . . . . . . . . . . . . Leduc(1878); Andraud
TELEMANN   Ouverture-Suite. Ed: ? . . . . . . . . . Andraud
TOMASI   Var. on a Corsican Theme. . . . . . . . . Leduc(1939); MBaron
TURECHEK   Intro. & Scherzo. . . . . . . . . . . . Witmark; MPHC
TUTHILL   Sailor's Hornpipe, Op 14#1 (1935). . . . . . . CFisch(1936); Andraud

WWQuint  cont.

VERRALL   Serenade for 5 Insts.  . . . . . . . . . . .   MusPr; Merc
WARD   Little Dance Suite. . . . . . . . . . . . . .   Mills
WATERSON   Quint--F. . . . . . . . . . . . . . . .   Lefleur(1922); Andraud
WEBER, C. M.   Rondo.   Arr: Kesnar. . . . . . . . .   Remick; MPHC
WEIS   Serenade. . . . . . . . . . . . . . . . . .   Hansen(1941)
WEISS   Quint (1932) . . . . . . . . . . . . . . . . . . . .
WOOD, CHAS.   Quint--F. . . . . . . . . . . . . .   Boosey(1933-34); Andraud
ZILCHER   Quint, Op 91. . . . . . . . . . . . . .   Müller(Heidelberg, 1894)
ZÖLLER   Quint--F, Op 132. . . . . . . . . . . .   Cubitt(London, 1883)


Misc:  5 Mixed Woodwinds

BOELLMANN   Gothic Minuet.   Ob, EH, Cl, Bn, Hn. . . . . .   Durand; E-V
CARTER   Quintet (1948).   5 Woodwinds. . . . . . . . . . .
DITTERSDORF   3 Partitas.   2Ob, 2Hn, Bn.   Ed: ? . . . . .   McG & M
DOMANSKY   Quint.   [Fl, 2Cl, Bn, Hn ?]. . . . . . . .   Schmidt(Heilbronn, 1927)
            2nd Quint.   Fl, 2Cl, Bn, Hn. . . . . . . . .   Schmidt(Heilbronn, 1936); Andrau
FINE   Partita (1948).   5 Woodwinds. . . . . . . . . . .
HUGUES   Allegro scherzoso--D, Op 92.   2Fl, Ob, Cl, Bn. . .   Ricordi(1883)
KARG-ELERT   Quint--c mi, Op 30.   Ob, 2Cl, Bn, Hn. . . . .   Kahnt(1912); Andraud
SODERO   Morning Prayer; Valse Scherzo.   WWQuar, Hn(TenSx). . . .   AMP
VALLENTIN   Quint--G, Op 30.   Ob, Cl, Bn, 2Hn. . . . . .   Author publ(Duisburg, 1941)
VILLA-LOBOS   Quinteto para instrumentos de sopro (1928)
                Fl, Ob, EH, Cl, Bn. . . . . . .   Eschig(Paris)
WEBER, JOS.   Quint (1900).   Woodwinds. . . . . . . . . . . .


5 INSTS. :  5 Brass


2 Ct, Hn, Tb or Bar, Tuba

CORELLI   Serenata.   Arr: Taylor. . . . . . . . . . . .   Mills
EWALD   Quint--b flat mi, Op 5.  . . . . . . . . . . .   Belaiev(1911); Rubank(3rd mvt. )
PETYREK   Schlussmusik zum Erntedankfest. . . . . . . .   Ullmann(1940)


2 Ct, Hn(Tb), Tb or Bar, Tuba  (each item has the Hn substitution).

_____   Sonata from Bankelsangerlieder.  Ed: King.  . .  Mus f Brass; ECSch
ADSON   2 Ayres for Cornetts & Sagbuts.   Ed: King.  . .  Mus f Brass; ECSch
BACH, J. S.   Contrapunctus #1, "Art of Fugue."  Arr:  King. . Mus f Brass; ECSch
BRADE   Allmand & Gaillard.  Ed: King. . . . . . . . .  Mus f Brass; ECSch
CONVERSE   2 Lyric Pcs. , Op 106#1, 2.  . . . . . . . .  Rubank
FRANCK   2 Pavans.  Ed: King. . . . . . . . . . . . .  Mus f Brass; ECSch
GABRIELI   Canzona per sonare #1, 2, 4.  Ed: King. . . .  Mus f Brass; ECSch
GREP   Paduana.  Ed: King. . . . . . . . . . . . . .  Mus f Brass; ECSch
HOLBORNE   Honiesuckle; Night Watch.  Ed: King. . . . .  Mus f Brass; ECSch
            Fruit of Love; Heigh-Ho Holiday. . . . . .  Merc
HOVHANESS   Sharagan & Fugue. . . . . . . . . . . . .  Mus f Brass; ECSch
KING   Prelude & Fugue. . . . . . . . . . . . . . . .  Mus f Brass; ECSch
MONTEVERDI   Suite.  Ed: Beck. . . . . . . . . . . .  Merc, MBaron

## 2 Ct, Hn(Tb), Tb or Bar, Tuba cont.

| | | |
|---|---|---|
| PEZEL | Sonata #1, 2, 3. Ed: King. . . . . . . . . . . . | Mus f Brass; ECSch |
| | 6 Pcs. Ed: King. . . . . . . . . . . . . . . | Mus f Brass; ECSch |
| | 3 Pcs. Ed: King. . . . . . . . . . . . . . . | Mus f Brass; ECSch |
| PURCELL | Funeral Music for Queen Mary. Ed: King. . . . | Mus f Brass; ECSch |

## Ct, Hn(Ct), Tb, Bar, Tuba unless otherwise given.

| | | |
|---|---|---|
| DES PRES | Motet & Royal Fanfare. Arr: King. . . . . . . | Mus f Brass; ECSch |
| GLAZOUNOV | In Modo Religioso--Eb, Op 38. Arr: King. . . | Mus f Brass; ECSch |
| PALESTRINA | 3 Hymns. Arr: King. . . . . . . . . . | Mus f Brass; ECSch |
| | Ricercar del primo tono. Ed: King. . . . . | Mus f Brass; ECSch |
| REICHE | Sonata #7. Ct, Hn(Tb), Tb, Bar, Tuba. Ed: King. . | Mus f Brass; ECSch |
| | Sonata #15. No substitutes. Ed: ? . . . . . . | Merc, MBaron |
| | 2 Sonatas, #18, 24. Ed: King. . . . . . . . . . | Mus f Brass; ECSch |
| SUSATO | 4 Dances. Ed: King. . . . . . . . . . . . . | Mus f Brass; ECSch |

## 2 Ct, 3 Tb

| | | |
|---|---|---|
| MENDELSSOHN, F. | Hunter's Farewell. 2Tt, Tb(Tt), 2Tb. . | MBaron |
| PEZEL | Turm-musik, 18 selected pcs. Ed: Meyer. . . . . | B&H(1930); AMP |
| | 2 Suites. Ed: Schering, in D. d. T. . . . . . . . . | B&H(1906) |
| | Turmmusiken und Suiten #27. Ed: Rein. . . . . . | B&H(1940) |
| SCHEIN | Musical Banquet. Ed: ? . . . . . . . . . . . | MBaron |
| SPEER | Sonata. 2Zinken(Tt), 3Tb. Ed: Schultz, in Erbe dt. Mus. . . . | Nagel |

## Misc: 5 Brass

| | | |
|---|---|---|
| BERGSMA | Suite for Brass Quintet (1946). . . . . . . . . . . . . . . | |
| COWELL | Action in Brass (1943). 5 Brasses. . . . . . . . . . | Edit. Musicus |
| REICHE | Sonata #7. Ct, Hn(Tb), Tb, Bar, Tuba ad lib. Ed: King. . . | Mus f Brass |
| SIMON | 4 Quints, Op 26. 2Ct, 2Hn, Tb. (Also arr. for 6 or 7). . . . | Jurgenson(1901) |
| SANDERS | Quint--Bb. 2Ct(Tt), Hn, 2Tb(Bar). . . . . . . . . . | Merc, MBaron |
| | Quint--B (1942). 5 Brasses. [Same as above?] . . . . | CFisch |
| STOLTZER | Fantasia in hypodorian. 2Tb(Hn), 2Tb, Tuba. Ed: King. | Mus f Brass |

## 5 INSTS.: 5 Misc. Winds

| | | |
|---|---|---|
| EISLER | Quint, Op 4. 5 Winds. . . . . . . . . . . . . . . . . . . . . . | |
| FITELBERG | Quint. Fl, Ob, Cl, BsCl, Tb(Bn). . . . . . . . . | Balan(1931); MBaron |
| HENKEMANS | Quint. Winds. . . . . . . . . . . . . . . . . . . | |
| MOYZES | Quint--Bb, Op 17. 5 Winds. . . . . . . . . . . . | Simrock(1943) |
| MUFFAT | Suiten aus dem Blumenbüschlein. 5 Winds. Ed: Woehl. | Bärenreiter(1938) |
| SIEGMEISTER | Quint (1932). Winds. . . . . . . . . . . . . . . . . . . | |
| WEBER, LUDW. | Quint. Winds. . . . . . . . . . . . . . . . . . . . . . . | |

# SIX INSTRUMENTS

## 6 INSTS. : including 1 to 5 Winds

### 1 Wind, StrQuint  unless otherwise given.

BOCCHERINI   6 Sextuors, Op 15.  Fl, 2Vl, Va, 2Vc.  . . . . . . . . .
            Sextuor--Eb, Op 42#1.  Hn, 2Vl, Va, 2Vc.  . . . . . . . . .
BUNNING   Hirtenruf, Idyll.  With Hn ad lib.  . . . . . . .Oertel(1900)
ENGEL   Suite for Orch--Eb, Op posth. 1.  Arr: Cl, StrQuint.  . . . UE(1930)
GERNSHEIM   Divertimento--E, Op 55[53?].  With Fl.  . . . Hymnophon(1888)
GOUVY   1st Serenade--G, Op 82.  With Fl.  . . . . . . . Kistner (1890)
        2nd Serenade--f mi, Op 84.  With Fl.  . . . . . . Rahter(1892)
HANDEL   Concerto Grosso #10.  With Ob.  (See under 8 INSTS. )  . . . B-N
HASSE   Suite--a mi, Op 36a.  With Fl. . . . . . . . . Litolff(1933)
HOFMANN   Serenade--D, Op 65.  With Fl. . . . . . . . B&H(1888); B-N
JADASSOHN   Serenade--D, Op 80.  With Fl.  . . . . . . Kistner(1888)
KRETSCHMER   Sextet--G, Op 40.  With Fl.  . . . . . . Hymnophon(1889)
KRUG   Serenade--D, Op 34.  With Fl.  . . . . . . . . Hymnophon(1887)
MILFORD   Sextet, Op 18.  With Fl.  . . . . . . . . . OUP(c1938)
SATTER   Sextet--A, Op 109.  Bn, 2Vl, Va, 2Vc.  . . . . . . R. Forberg(1869)
STOLZENBERG   Serenade--d mi, Op 6.  With Cl. . . . . . B&H
WAGNER   Adagio.  With Cl. . . . . . . . . . . . . B&H; McG & M


### 2 Winds, StrQuar

BAUER   Concertino, Op 32b (1939).  With Ob, Cl. * . . . . . Arrow(1943)
BEETHOVEN   Sextet--Eb, Op 81b (1795).  With 2Hn. . . . . B&H; AMP, MBaron
HERRMANN, ED.   Sextet--g mi, Op 33.  With Ob, Cl.  . . . Raabe & Plothow(1916)
IRELAND   Sextet.  With Cl, Hn. . . . . . . . . . . . . . . . . .
KUBIK   Trivialities, Op 5 (1934).  With Fl, Hn. . . . . . . . . .
REICHA   Sextet.  With 2Cl.  . . . . . . . . . . . . . . . . . .


### Misc: including 2 Winds

HAUER   7 Var. , Op 35.  Fl, Cl, Vl, Va, Vc, Cb. . . . . . . . . . . . .
JAUNEZ   Sextuor--A, Op 4.  2Hn, 2Vl, 2Va.  . . . . . . . Costallat
TOCH   Tanzsuite, Op 30.  Fl, Cl, Vl, Va, Cb, Perc. . . . . . Schott(1924)


### Misc: including 3 Winds

BOCCHERINI   Sextuor, Op 42#2.  Fl(Ob), Bn, Hn, Vl, Va, Cb.  . . . . . .
CHOULET   Sextuor, Op 18.  Fl, Ob, Hn, Vl, Vc, Cb. . . . . . Costallat(1845)
DELLO JOIO   Sextet (1943).  3Recorders(WW), 3Str. . . . . . Hargail
ERLANGER   Sextet--Eb, Op 41.  Cl, Bn, Hn, Vl, Va, Vc. . . . Kistner(1882)
IBERT   Gardener of Samos.  Fl, Cl, Tt, Vl, Vc, Perc. . . . . Heugel(1935); Andraud
JAUNEZ   Sextuor--E, Op 5.  Fl, 2Hn, Vl, 2Vc. . . . . . . . Costallat
LUENING   Sextet, Op 2 (1919).  Fl, Cl, Hn, Vl, Va, Vc.. . . . . . .
MARX   18 Var. on an Old English Folksong, Op 30.
          2Fl, Ob(Vl), Vl, Va, Vc.  . . . . . . . Bärenreiter(1938)
STICH   Sextet.  Cl, Bn, Hn, Vl, Va, Cb. . . . . . . . . . .

*Cb part also available, playable as Str. Orch.

Misc: including 3 Winds  cont.

STÖHR   Sextet--E, Op 2.  Cl, 2Hn, Vl, Va, Vc. . . . . . . .   Eulenburg(1888)
WAGNER-REGENY   Kleine Gemeinschaftsmusik--C.
                        Ob, Cl, Bn, Vl, Va, Vc. . . . . .   UE(1929)


Misc: including 4 Winds

DONDERER   Suite.   4 Natural Tt, 2Perc. . . . . . . . .   B&H(1940)
ROUSSELOT   Sextet.   Ob, Cl, Bn, Hn, Vc, Cb. . . . . . . .   Catelin(Paris)


## 6 INSTS.:  6 Winds

WWQuint, 1 additional Wind

ACHRON   Sextet, Op 73 (1938).  Plus Tt. . . . . . . . . .   NME XV#4(1942)
BOSSI   Tema variato, Op 10a.  Plus Tt. . . . . . . . .   Böhm(1939)
DEVASINI   Sextet.  Plus Cl. . . . . . . . . . . .   Ricordi(1843)
JANACEK   Mlade, Suite (1924).  Plus BsCl. . . . . . .   Hudebni Matice(1925); Andraud
KLEINSINGER   Design for WW.  Plus Cl. . . . . . . . .   Broadcast; AMP, MBaron
LEFEBVRE   2nd Suite, Op 122.  Plus Cl. . . . . . . . .   Andraud
MALHERBE   Sextet.  Plus EH. . . . . . . . . . . .   Ms at Curtis
MAPES   Passacaglia.  Plus EH. . . . . . . . . . . .   Ms at Curtis
REINECKE   Sextet--Bb, Op 271.  Plus Hn. . . . . . . . .   Zimmerman(1904); Andraud
SCHERRER   Old French Dances, Op 11.  [Op II ?].  Plus Cl.   Andraud
THOMSON   Barcarolle for WW.  Fl, EH, Cl, Bn, Hn, BsCl. . .   Merc


6 Woodwinds:  2 Ob, 2 Bn, 2 Hn

HAYDN   Divertimento--C.  Ed: Sandberger. . . . . . . .   Sandberger, jr. (Munich, 1935)
MOZART   Contradance in Rondo Form.  Ed: ? . . . . . .   Marks
         Divertimento #8--F,  K 213 (1775).  . . . . . .   B&H(1880); AMP, Andraud
         Divertimento #9--Bb,  K 240 (1776).  . . . . . .   B&H(1880)
         Divertimento #12--Eb,  K 252 (1776).  . . . . . .   B&H(1880)
         Divertimento #13--F,  K 253 (1776).  . . . . . .   B&H(1880)
         Divertimento #14--Bb,  K 270 (1777).  . . . . . .   B&H(1880)
         Divertimento #16--Eb,  K 289 (1777).  . . . . . .   B&H(1880)


6 Woodwinds:  2 Cl, 2 Bn, 2 Hn

BEETHOVEN   March--Bb, bef. Op 1.  In Werke, Ser. V#33  .   B&H(1864-87)
            Sextet--Eb, Op 71 (1792-97).  . . . . . . .   B&H(1864); AMP, IMC
            Minuet & March. . . . . . . . . . . . .   Marks
MOZART   Serenade #11--Eb, K 375 (1787). . . . . . . . .   B&H(1880)


6 Woodwinds:  6 Saxes

GUILMANT, (A. ?) Cantilene Pastorale.  Arr:  3AltSx, 2TenSx, BarSx by Taylor. . .  Mills
SCHUBERT, FR.  March Militaire.  Arr:  3AltSx, TenSx, BarSx, BsSx by Holmes. . .  Rubank
SUPPE   Poet & Peasant.  Arr:  3AltSx, TenSx, BarSx, BsSx. . . . . . . . . . .  Rubank

## 6 Brass:  2 Ct, Hn, Tb, Bar(Tb), Tuba

BACH, J. S.    Contrapunctus #3 from Art of Fugue.  Arr: King. . . . Mus f Brass
BECKER   Romance. . . . . . . . . . . . . . . . . . . . Remick
BENOIST   Fantasie l'Amerique. . . . . . . . . . . . . . . CFisch
BOROWSKY   Moods; Twilight Hymn.  . . . . . . . . . . . . Boosey
CLAPP   Circus Day, Moonlight Dance, Prelude-Pastoral (1937?). . Boosey
CONVERSE, (F. S. ?)   Prelude & Intermezzo, Op 103#1. . . . . . . Boosey
COWELL   Tell Tale . . . . . . . . . . . . . . . . . Merc, MBaron
DAHL   Music for Brass Insts.  . . . . . . . . . . . . Witmark; MPHC
FRANCK   2 Intradas.  Arr: Long. . . . . . . . . . . . . Rubank
GOUNOD   Soldiers Chos. from Faust.  Arr: Gordon. . . . . . . Witmark; MPHC
HAUBIEL   Ballade. . . . . . . . . . . . . . . . . . . CompPr
KESSEL   Sonata mit blasenden Instrumenten.  Ed: King. . . . . . Mus f Brass
SOMMER & HARDING  2 Dances (on the same theme).  Arr:  King. . . Mus f Brass
TALLMADGE   Rain; Frontier.  . . . . . . . . . . . . . Witmark; MPHC
TSCHAIKOWSKY  Capriccio Italien.  Arr: Tallmadge. . . . . . . Boosey (?)
WAGNER   Prelude Act III "Die Meistersinger. "  Arr. . . . . . . Boosey
          King's Prayer, Finale,"Lohengrin"Act I.  Arr: Schaefer. Broadcast; AMP
          Excerpts from"Parsifal";"Tannhauser. "  Arr.  . . . . Pro-Art

## 6 Brass:  3 Tt, 3 Tb

FRANCK   Intrada.  Ed: Rein. . . . . . . . . . . . . . . B&H
HASTETTER   Musik um Weihnachten. . . . . . . . . . . . B&H(1940)
MARX   Turmmusik, Op 37#1.  . . . . . . . . . . . . Bärenreiter(1942)
SCHMID   Trum-musik, Op 105. . . . . . . . . . . . . B&H(1940)
WÜRZ   Turmmusik. . . . . . . . . . . . . . . . . B&H(1940)

## Misc:  6 Brass

BÖHME   Sextet--e mi, Op 30 (1911).   Ct, 2Tt, BsTt(Hn), Tb(TenHn), Tuba(Bar).
                                      . . . . . . . . Böhme(Rostock, 1913)
          ditto . . .  3Tt, Hn, Tb, Tuba. . . . . . . . . . . Witmark; MPHC
DAUPRAT   Sextuor, Op 10.  6Hn. . . . . . . . . . . . Lemoine(c1840)
KIESSIG   5 Stücke, Op 57#1.  2Tt, 2Hn, Tb, Tuba. . . . . . . Portius(1937)
RUGGLES   Angels, from "Men & Angels. "  6 muted Tt. . . . . . Curwen(1925)
SIMON   Sextet.   See Brass Quint, Op 26.
          4 Pcs. for Sextet, Op 26#15-18.   2Tt, Hn, Hn(Bar), Tb, Tb(Tuba).
                    Ed: Voxman.  . . . . . . . . . Rubank

## 6 Misc. Winds

BUMCKE   Sextet--Ab, Op 19.   EH, Cl, BsCl, Bn, Sx, Waldhorn.  . . . Diem(1908)
FICHER   Suite en Estilo Antiquo (1930).  6 Winds. . . . . . . . .
KARREN   Humoristic Scenes.  Fl, Ob, Cl, BsCl, CBn, Hn. . . . . . . Andraud
MEL-BONIS   Sextet.  Winds. . . . . . . . . . . . . . . . .
PROWO   Concerto--C.   2BsTt, 2Ob, 2Bn.  Ed: Schultz, in Erbe dt. Mus. . . Nagel
ROSETTI   Parthia--Bb.  Ob, 2Cl, Bn, 2Hn.  Ed: Kaul, In D. T. B. XXXIII. . . B&H

## 1 Wind, StrQuar, Pf(Hp)

ACHRON   Children's Suite, Op 57.  With Cl.   . . . . . . . . .   UE(1928); Andraud
BACH, J. S.   Suite--b mi.  With Fl.  (Usually perf. as StrOrch). . .   Schott; AMP
BAX   In Memoriam.  With EH, uses Hp.   . . . . . . . . . . .   Murdoch(1935)
BEREZOWSKY   Fantastic Var. --Ab, Op 7 (1926).  With Cl.  . .   Russ. M-V(1935); Andraud
COPLAND   Arr. of "Short Symphony"(1937).  With Cl.   . . . . . . . . .
DAHLHOFF   Der Marchenerzahler.  With Fl, uses Hp ad lib.  . . . . . . . . . .
DOUGLAS, KEITH   Sea Wrack.  With Fl, uses Hp.  . . . . . . . . . .
HANDEL   Ob Concerti #1, 3--Bb, F.  In Werke XXI.   . . . . . . .   B&H(1858)
HARRIS   Concerto (1927).  With Cl.   . . . . . . . . . . . .   CosCob(1932); Arrow
HOLBROOKE   4 Dances, Op 20.  With Cl.   . . . . . . . . . .   Ricordi
MARINUZZI   Andante all'Antica.  With Fl, uses Hp ad lib.   . . . .   B-N
MASON   3 Pcs., Op 13 (1911-12, rev. 1943).  With Fl, uses Hp.   . .   SPAM(1923, '43); GSch
McKAY   April Poem (1931).  With Fl.  . . . . . . . . . . . . . .
PETYREK   Sextet.  With Cl. . . . . . . . . . . . . . . . .   UE(1924); Peters
POLSTERER   Sextet.  With Ob.  . . . . . . . . . . . . . .   Brockhaus(1925)
PROKOVIEV   Overture on Yiddish Themes, Op 34.  With Cl.  . . .   B&H(1922); AMP, IMC
RAWLINGS   Chamber Concerto.  With Fl.  . . . . . . . . . .   Chappell
SCHISKE   Sextet.  With Cl.  . . . . . . . . . . . . . . .   UE(1940)
STILLMAN   Fantasy on a chassidish theme.  With Cl.   . . . . .   UE(1932)
TELEMANN   Concerto.  With Fl.  Ed: ? . . . . . . . . . . . .   Andraud
WEBER, EDM.   Sextet--Eb, Op 35.  With Hn.  . . . . . . . . .   Bosworth(1886)

## Misc:  including 1 Wind & Pf

FAUCONIER   Sextuor.  Fl, 2Vl, Vc, Cb, Pf. . . . . . . . . . .   Schott(1875)
   Sextuor #2--a mi.  Fl, 2Vl, Vc, Cb, Pf.  . . . . . . . . . . . .
HANDEL   Concerto Grosso #9.  Ob, 2Vl, Vc, 2Pf. . . . . . . .   B-N

## Misc:  including 2 Winds & Pf(Hp)

BACH, J. C.   Quints--C, G, F, Eb, A, D; Op 11.  Fl, Ob(Vl), Vl, Va, Vc, Pf.
   Ed: Steglich. . . . . .   Nagel(1936)
DOHNANYI   Sextet--C, Op 57.  Cl, Hn, Vl, Va, Vc, Pf.  . . . . .   Lengnick; Mills
HAYDN   Capriccio.  Fl, Cl, Vl, Va, Vc, Hp.  Ed: Tocchi. . . . .   DeSantis(1940)
HIMMEL   Sextet, Op 19.  2Hn, 2Va, Vc, Pf.  . . . . . . . . .   Erard & Pleyel
KALKBRENNER   Sextet--f mi, Op 135.  2Hn, Vl, Vc, Cb, Pf. . . . . . . . . . . .f . . . .
PONFICK   Sextuor--A, Op 8.  2Hn, Vl, Va, Vc, Pf.  . . . . . . .   Ries & Erler(c1879)
SCARLATTI, A.   Sonata.  2Fl, 2Vl, Continuo(Pf & Vc). . . . . . . . . . . . . . . . . .

## Misc:  including 3 Winds & Pf(Hp, Hpschd)

EMMANUEL   Trois airs rhythmes.  2Fl, EH, Vc, 2Hp.  . . . . . .   Hayet(c1905)
deFALLA   Concerto de Camera (1923-26).
   Hpschd Solo(Pf), Fl, Ob, Cl, Vl, Vc. . . . . . . .   Eschig(1928)
MARTINU   La Revue de Cuisine.  Cl, Bn, Tt, Vl, Vc, Pf.  . . . . .   Leduc; MBaron
OSBORNE, G. A.   Sextet--E, Op 63.  Fl, Ob, Hn, Vc, Cb, Pf.  . . . .   Lemoine(1847)
RIES   Sextet for Pf & Hp--g mi, Op 142.  Pf, Hp, Cl, Bn, Hn, Cb. . . .   Schott(1879)

## Misc:  including 4 Winds & Pf

ONSLOW    Sextet--Eb,  Op 30.    Fl, Cl, Hn, Bn, Cb, Pf.  . . . . . . .   B&H; AMP
          Sextet--a mi,  Op 77b.   Fl, Cl, Hn, Bn, Cb, Pf.  . . . . . .   Kistner(1851)


## WWQuint, Pf

BLUMER    Original Th. & Var. --F, Op 45. . . . . . . . . . .   Simrock(1922); AMP
BRAUER    Sextet--g mi. . . . . . . . . . . . . . . . . . .   B&H(1920); AMP
BRUNEAU   Sextuor--C. . . . . . . . . . . . . . . . . . .   Schneider(Paris, 1904)
BULLERIAN    Sextet--Gb, Op 38. . . . . . . . . . . . . . .   Simrock(1925); AMP
DAVID, J. N.    Divertimento, Op 24.   Ed:  Bohle. . . . . . . . .   B&H(1940)
DESPORTES    Prelude & Pastorale. . . . . . . . . . . . . .   Andraud
DUKELSKY    Nocturne. . . . . . . . . . . . . . . . . . .   CFisch(1947)
FUHRMEISTER    Gavotte & Tarantelle, Op 6. . . . . . . . . .   Andraud
GENIN, T. jr.    Sextuor--Eb. . . . . . . . . . . . . . . .   Eschig(1906); Andraud
HARRIS    Sextet (1932). . . . . . . . . . . . . . . . . . . . .   .
HILL, E. B.    Sextet--Bb, Op 39 (1934). . . . . . . . . . .   SPAM(1938); GSch
HOLBROOKE    Sextet--f mi, Op 33a. . . . . . . . . . . . . .   Chester(1906); Andraud
HUBER    Sextet--Bb.  . . . . . . . . . . . . . . . . .   Hug(1924)
d'INDY    Sarabande & Menuet--D & d, Op 72 (1918).
               Arr. from Suite for Pf, Op 24 (1885).  . . . . .   Hamelle; Andraud
JENTSCH    Theme & Var. . . . . . . . . . . . . . . . . .   Ries & Erler(1935-36)
JONGEN    Rhapsodie. Op 70. . . . . . . . . . . . . . . .   Andraud
JUON    Divertimento--F, Op 51. . . . . . . . . . . . . .   Lienau(1913); ECSch
KOPPEL    Sekstet, Op 36. . . . . . . . . . . . . . . . .   McG & M
LACROIX    Sextet. . . . . . . . . . . . . . . . . . . .   Ms at Curtis
MIROUZE    Sextet [?]. . . . . . . . . . . . . . . . . .   Leduc(1933)
POULENC    Sextuor.  . . . . . . . . . . . . . . . . . .   McG & M, Andraud
QUEF    Sextet, Op 4. . . . . . . . . . . . . . . . . .   Noël(Paris, c1920)
REUCHSEL    Sextet--G. . . . . . . . . . . . . . . . . .   Lemoine(1909)
RHEINBERGER    Sextet--F, Op 191b. . . . . . . . . . . . .   Leuckart; Andraud
RICCI-SIGNORINI    Fantasia burlesca--C. . . . . . . . . . .   Carisch(1925)
RIETZ    Concertstück, Op 41.  . . . . . . . . . . . . .   Andraud
ROUSSEL    Divertissement--G, Op 6 (1905). . . . . . . . .   Rouart(1906); MBaron
TANSMAN    Witches Dance, from Garden of Paradise. . . . . .   Eschig; AMP
THUILLE    Sextet--Bb, Op 6.  . . . . . . . . . . . . . .   B&H(1889); AMP
          ditto . . . Gavotte only. . . . . . . . . . . .   CFisch
TUTHILL    Var. on When Johnny Comes Marching Home, Op 9 (1934). . .   Galaxy
VELLONES    A Versailles. . . . . . . . . . . . . . . . .   MBaron
WEISS    Sextet.   Woodwinds, Hn, Pf. . . . . . . . . . . . . . . . .


## Misc:  5 Winds, Pf

BRETON    Sextet for 5 Wind Insts.   5 Winds, Pf.  . . . . . .   Union Music. Espanola(1900?)
DONOVAN    Sextet (1932).  Winds, Pf. . . . . . . . . . . . . . . . . .
DRESDEN    3 Sextets.  Winds, Pf. . . . . . . . . . . . . . . . . . .
FISCHER    Suites #3-6--Bb, d mi, G, F.   Ed: Woehl. . . . . . .   Bärenreiter(1939)
LEYE    Sextet, Op 3.   Fl, Basset Hn(Cl), Bn, 2Hn, Pf.  . . . . .   Sinner(Coburg, 1844)
PIJPER    Sextet.  Winds, Pf. . . . . . . . . . . . . . . . . . . .
TARTINI, (G. ?).    Largo from Sonata--g mi.   Arr: Fl, Ob, 2Cl, Hn, Pf. . . .   Witmark
VINEE    Sextet.  Winds, Pf.  . . . . . . . . . . . . . . . . . . .

# SEVEN INSTRUMENTS

## 7 INSTS. : including 1 to 6 Winds

### 2 Winds: StrQuint, 2 Hn

| | | |
|---|---|---|
| MOZART | Divertimento #7--D, K 205 (1773). . . . . . . . | B&H(1880); AMP |
| | Divertimento #10--F, K 247 (1776). . . . . . . . | Heckel(1852), B&H; AMP |
| | Divertimento #15--Bb, K 287 (1777). . . . . . . | Heckel(1852), B&H; AMP |
| | Divertimento #17--D, K 334 (1779). . . . . . . | Heckel(1852), B&H; IMC |
| PLEYEL | Septet. . . . . . . . . . . . . . . | Sieber |

### 3 Winds: 3 Winds, StrQuar

BLISS  Septet.  With Fl, Ob, Bn. . . . . . . . . . . . . Andraud
COPPOLA  5 Poemes.  With Fl, Cl, Tt. . . . . . . . . . . Durand(1933)
d'INDY  Suite dans le style ancien, for Tt--D, Op 24 (1886).
                   For Tt, with 2Fl. . . . . . Hamelle(1887); IMC
TIESSEN  Septet--G, Op 20 (1914-15).  With Fl, Cl, Hn. . . . . . . . . .

### 3 Winds: with Vl, Va, Vc, Cb

BEETHOVEN  Septet--Eb, Op 20 (bef. 1800).  Cl, Bn, Hn. . . B&H; IMC, Peters
BERWALD  Septet--Bb (1828).  Cl, Bn, Hn. . . . . . Musik. Konstför(Stockholm, 1883)
BLANC  Septuor--E, Op 40.  Cl, Bn, Hn. . . . . . . . . Costallat
KREUTZER, KONR.  Septuor--Eb, Op 62.  Cl, Bn, Hn. . . . . . . . . . .
MILHAUD  Symph. #2, "Pastorale"(1918).  Fl, EH, Bn.  . . . UE(1922); Merc
          Symph. #3, "Serenade"(1921).  Fl, Cl, Bn. . . . . UE(1922); Andraud
MOZART  Divertimento #7--D, K 205 (1773).  Bn, 2Hn*. . .

### 4 Winds

BEETHOVEN  11 Viennese Dances (1819).
                   2Fl(Cl), 2Hn, 2Vl, Bs(incl. Bn in one mvt. ). . . B&H(1907)
POPOW  Septuor, Op 2.  Fl&Picc, Cl, Bn, Tt, Vl, Vc, Cb. . . . . . . UE(1928)
STRAVINSKY  L'histoire d'un soldat.  Vl, Cl, Bn, Tt, Tb, Cb, Drum . . Philharmonia; AMP
WEBER, JOS. M.  Aus meinem Leben--E.  Vl, Va, Vc, Cl, Bn, 2Hn . . UE(1899); Andraud
WELLESZ  Dance Suite.  Vl Solo, Va, Vc, Fl, Cl, EH, Bn. . . . . . . . . . . . . . .

### 5 Winds

MONTEAUX  Arietta & March.  WWQuar, Tt, Cb, Perc. . . . Mathot; Andraud
VILLA-LOBOS  Choros #7.  WWQuar, Sx, Vl, Vc. . . . . . . Eschig, Schott(1928)

---

*Though published for StrQuint, 2Hn, Mozart wrote this for Vl, Va, Bs, 2Hn, Bn, with the Bn doubling the Bs line.  See Einstein Mozart, p. 197.

## 6 Winds: 6 Winds, 1 Perc

JANSSEN   Obsequies of a Saxophone.   6 Winds, SnareDr. . . . . . . . . . .
MARCELLI   Music Box.   Picc, 2Fl, Ob, 2Cl, Bells. . . . . . . . . . .   Mills
MOZART   Divertimento #5, 6--C, C; K 187, 188 (1773).
                   Arr: 2Cl, 3Tt, Tb, Tymp by Kahn. . . . . . . .   Marks
TSCHAIKOWSKY   Capriccio Italien, Op 45 (1880).
                   Arr: 2Tt, Hn, Bar, Tb, Tuba, Marimba by Talmadge. . . Belwin
              Intro. & Finale from Swan Lake, Op 20 (1876).
                   Arr: 2Tt, Hn, Bar, Tb, Tuba, Marimba by Talmadge. . . Belwin
VERDI   Triumphal March from Aida (1871).
                   Arr: 2Tt, 2Hn, Tb(Bar), Tuba, Tymp by Gordon. . .   Witmark; MPHC

## 7 INSTS. :   7 Winds

## WWQuar, 3 additional Woodwinds

BOLZONI   Minuetto.   Plus Cl, AltCl, BsCl.   Arr: Conn. . . . . .   CFisch
BUSCH   Ozark Reverie.   Plus Cl, 2Hn. . . . . . . . . . . .   Fitzsimmons
DALLEY   Serenade.   Plus Fl, Cl, Bn. . . . . . . . . . .   Witmark; MPHC
FLAMENT   Fantasia con fugua, Op 28.   Plus EH, 2Hn. . . . . .   Andraud
HABERT   Scherzo, Op 107.   Plus Bn, 2Hn. . . . . . . . .   B&H; AMP
d'INDY   Chanson et Danses--Bb, Op 50 (1898).   Plus Cl, Hn, Bn. . . Durand(1899); E-V
MOUQUET   Adagio, Aubade, Scherzo.   Plus Cl, Bn, Hn. . . . . . Lemoine(1910); Andraud
PIERNE, GABR.   Preludio & Fughetta--c mi, Op 40.   Plus Fl, Bn, Hn. Hamelle(1906); Andraud
RHENE-BATON   Aubade, Op 53.   Plus Cl, Bn, Hn. . . . . . .   Durand; E-V
RÖNTGEN   Serenade--A, Op 14.   Plus Bn, 2Hn. . . . . . . .   B&H(1878)
SCHUMANN   Knight Rupert, from Album for Young for Pf, Op 68#12.
                   Arr: plus Cl, AltCl, BsCl by Cheyette-Roberts .   CFisch
TOJA   Serenata.   Plus Cl, 2Hn. . . . . . . . . . . . . .   Ricordi
WIND   Serenade Amusante, Op 1339.   Plus Cl, 2Hn. . . . . . .   Andraud

## Misc: 7 Woodwinds

BACH, K. P. E.   6 Sonatas--G, F, A, D, Eb, C.   2Fl, 2Cl, Bn, 2Hn. Ed: Leupold . . Litolff(1935-37)
RAMEAU   Musette en Rondeau.   Arr: 3Cl, 2Bn, 2Hn. . . . . . . . . . .   Andraud
           Tambourin.   Arr: 3Cl, 2Bn, 2Hn. . . . . . . . . . . . .   Andraud
ROSETTI   Parthia--D.   2Ob, 2Cl, Bn, 2Hn.   Ed: Kaul, in D. T. B. XXXIII. . .   B&H

## Misc: 7 Brass

BEREZOWSKY   Suite, Op 24 (1938).   2Tt, 2Hn, 2Tb, Tuba. . . . .   Mills
BRABEC   Bläsermusiken.   2Tt, 3Hn, 2Tb. . . . . . . . . . . .   Ullman(1940)
BUONAMENTE   Sonata.   Arr: 2Ct, 2Hn, Tb, Bar, Tuba by King. . . .   Mus f Brass
COHN   Music for Brass Insts.   3Tt, Tt(Hn), 2Tb, BsTb. . . . . .   SMPC
KOMMA   Musik. For 7 Brasses. . . . . . . . . . . . . . .   Ullmann(1940)
LECAIL   Septet for Brass.   Tts, Tbs. . . . . . . . . . . . .   Evette & Schaeffer(1921)
LOCKE   Music for King Chas. II.   Arr: 3Ct, Hn(Tb), Tb, Bar, Tuba. .   Mus f Brass
OSBORNE, WILLS.   Prelude.   2Ct, Ct(Hn), Tb(Hn), Tb, Bar, Tuba. .   Mus f Brass
              2 Ricercari.   2Ct, 2Hn, Tb, Bar, Tuba. . . . .   Mus f Brass
RUGGLES   Angels, from "Men and Angels."   4 muted Tt, 3 muted Tb. . . . . . NME
SCHEIN   Gagliarda.   Brass Septet[?].   Ed: ? . . . . . . . . .   McG & M
SEEBOTH   Suite.   4Tt, 3Tb. . . . . . . . . . . . . . .   Heinrichshofen(1940)
SIMON   Brass Septet.   See Brass Quint, Op 26.

FLEISCHER    Konzert--F#.    StrQuint, Fl, Cl.  . . . . . . . . . . . .  Schultheiss(1935)
HINDEMITH    Septet for Wind Insts. (1948).  WWQuint, BsCl, Tt.. . . . . . .  Schott; AMP
MAYR, S.    In the Morning.   Fl, Ob, 2Cl, 2Bn, Tt(Hn). . . . . . . . . . .  Andraud
MOZART    Serenade #10--Bb, K 361 (1780).   Arr: Ob, 2Cl, 2AltCl, Bn, Cb.   Andraud
PIERNE, GABR.    Pastorale Variee--Bb,  Op 30.
                                Fl, Ob, Cl, 2Bn, Tt, Hn. . . . . . . . . .  Durand; E-V
ROSETTI    Parthia--F.   3Ob, 2Hn, Bn, Violone.
                                Ed: Kaul, in D. T. B. XXXIII.  . . . . . . .  B&H(1925)
WOOD, CHAS.    Septet.   Winds & Strs.  . . . . . . . . . . . . . . . . . .


## 7 INSTS. :  including Pf(Keyboard, etc. )

1 Wind:  with StrQuint, Pf(Hp)  unless otherwise given.

BAX    An Irish Elegy (1917).    EH, uses Hp.  . . . . . . . . . . .
DUVERNOY    Serenade--Eb.   Tt. . . . . . . . . . . . .  Heugel(bef. 1892); Andraud
HANDEL    Concerto Grosso #8.   Ob, 4Str, 2Pf. . . . . . .  B-N
d'INDY    Concert, Op 89.    Fl, Vc, Pf;StrQuar(StrOrch).  . .  Andraud
KUBINSKY    Legende (1943?).   Cl, uses Hp.  . . . . . .  Krenn(1944)
SAINT-SAENS    Septet--Eb, Op 65 (1881).   Tt.  . . . . . .  Durand(1881); E-V,  IMC
SEVERAC    Serenade au clair de la lune.   Fl.  . . . . . .  Lointier(Nice, 1893)
           Le Parc aux cerfs.   Ob.  . . . . . . . . . . . . . . . .


2 Winds:  with StrQuar, Pf(Hp)  unless otherwise given.

BACH, K. P. E.    6 Sonatas--G, F, A, D, Eb, C.   2Fl.   Ed: Leupold . . . . . .  Litolff(1935-37)
             Sonatine--C, 2Fl.  Ed: v. Dameck.  . . . . .  Raabe & Plothow(1922); Andraud
BAX    Concerto (1934).   Fl, Ob; uses Hp. . . . . . . . . . . . . .
FESCA    2 Septets--c mi, d mi; Op 26, 28.   Ob, Hn, Vl, Va, Vc, Cb, Pf. . . . .  Litolff(c1842)
HOLLANDER, BENO.    Sextet--Eb, Op 28.   2Hn . . . . . . . . .  Phillips & Page(c1900)
MEL-BONIS    Septet.   2Fl. . . . . . . . . . . . . . . . . . . . . . . .
MOSCHELES    Septet--D, Op 88.   Cl, Hn, Vl, Va, Vc, Cb, Pf. . . . . . . . .  Kistner
RAVEL    Intro. & Allegro--Gb (1906).   Fl, Cl; uses Hp.
             [Scored for Orch., sometimes played as Septet] . . . . .  Durand(1906)


3 Winds:  with Vl, Va, Vc, Pf(Hp)

BACH, FRIEDR.    Septet--c mi, Op 3.   Ob, 2Hn.   Ed: Schünemann . . . . .  Kistner(1920)
GENZMER    Septet.   Fl, Cl, Hn; uses Hp. . . . . . . . . . . . .  Schott; AMP
GHEDINI    Adagio e Allegro di Concerto.   Fl, Cl, Hn; uses Hp. . . . . . .  Ricordi(1937)
HABA    Septet, Op 16.   Cl, Bn, Hn.  . . . . . . . . . . . . . . . . .  Andraud
SCHÖNBERG    Suite, Op 29 (1934).   KleineCl(Picc), Cl, BsCl(Bn) . . . . . .  UE(1926)
STEINBACH    Septet--A, Op 7.   Ob, Cl, Hn. . . . . . . . . . . . . . .  Schott(1882)


3 Winds:  misc., including Pf(Hp)

HUMMEL    Septuor--d mi, Op 74.   Fl, Ob, Hn, Va, Vc, Cb, Pf. . . . . . . . .  Schott(1869)
          ditto .  .   Some editions are:  Fl, Ob, Hn, Bn, Vc, Cb, Pf. . . . . . . . . . .
          Military Septet--C, Op 114.   Fl, Cl, Tt, Vl, Vc, Cb, Pf . . . . . .  Haslinger(1878)
JANACEK    Concertino (1926).   Cl, Bn, Hn, 2Vl, Va, Pf.  . . . .  Hudebni Matice(1926); Andraud
KRUMPHOLTZ    2 Symphonies for Hp.   Hp, Fl, 2Hn, 2Vl, Vc. . . . . . . . . . .
RIES    Septet--Eb, Op 25 (1808).   Cl, 2Hn, Vl, Vc, Cb, Pf.  . . . . . . . .  Simrock

## 4 Winds:  with 2 Str.  Pf

BLANC   Septuor--E, Op 54 (c1864).   Fl, Ob, Cl, Hn, Vc, Cb, Pf. .  .  .  .   Costallat(c1870)
HUMMEL   Septuor--d mi, Op 74.   See above 3Winds: misc. , incl.  Pf.
KALKBRENNER   Septet--A, Op 132.   Ob, Cl, Hn, Bn, Vc, Cb, Pf. .  .  .   B&H
SPOHR   Septet--A, Op 147.   Fl, Cl, Bn, Hn, Vl, Vc, Pf. .  .  .  .  .  .  .  .   Peters(1855); Andraud

## 5 Winds:  WWQuint, Pf, 1 additional inst. unless otherwise given.

BOISDEFFRE   Scherzo--Bb, Op 49.   Plus Cb ad lib. .  .  .  .  .  .  .  .   Hamelle(1894; Andraud
DOST   Septet--G, Op 55.   Plus Perc. .  .  .  .  .  .  .  .  .  .  .  .   Zimmerman(1923)
FASANOTTI   Settimino--Eb.   Ob, Cl, 2Bn, Hn, Vc, Pf. .  .  .  .  .  .  .   Ricordi(1842)
KITTL   Septet--Eb, Op 25.   Plus Cb.   .  .  .  .  .  .  .  .  .  .  .   Kistner(1846)
ONSLOW   Septet--Bb, Op 79.   Plus Cb. .  .  .  .  .  .  .  .  .  .  .   Kistner(1852)
PIERNE, GABR.   March of Little Tin Soldiers.   Arr.; plus Perc. .  .   Leduc; Andraud
PIJPER   Septet.   Plus Cb. .  .  .  .  .  .  .  ..  .  .  .  .  .  .  .  .  .  .  .  .

## 6 Winds:  with Hp(Organ)

BUMCKE   Von Liebe und Leid, Op 24.   WWQuar, 2Hn, Hp. .  .  .  .  .  .   Diem(1 913)
SAINT-MARTIN   In Memoriam.   3Tt, 3Tb, Organ.   .  .  .  .  .  .  .  .   Durand; E-V

# EIGHT INSTRUMENTS

## 3 Winds, with StrQuint unless otherwise given.

DUPUY   Serenata.   With Fl, Ob, Bn. . . . . . . . . . . . Author publ. (Paris, 1897)
        Une soiree d'ete, Elegie.  With Fl, Ob, Bn. . . . . Author publ. (Paris)
FERGUSON   Octet (1933).  With Cl, Bn, Hn. . . . . . . . Boosey(1934)
KAUN, HUGO   Octet--F, Op 34.  With Cl, Bn, Hn. . . . . Rühle(1892)
LACHMANN, (R. ?)  Hungarian Minuet.  With Fl, Cl, Bn. . . Andraud
MIRANDOLLE   Oktett--D.  With Cl, Bn, Hn. . . . . . . Author publ. (Haag, 1944)
MOLBE   Octet--F, Op 20.  With Cl, Bn, Hn. . . . . . . . Hofmeister(1897)
        Octet--d mi, Op 45.  With Ob, BassetHn, Hn.  . . . Hofmeister(1898)
        Serenade--Bb, Op 46.  With Ob, BassetHn, Hn.. . . Hofmeister(1897)
        Octet--G, Op 47.  With Cl, EH, Bn.  . . . . . . Hofmeister(1898)
MOZART   Divertimento #11--D, K 251 (1776).  Ob, 2Hn. . . B&H(1880); AMP
SCHUBERT, FR.  Octet--F, Op 166 (1824).  Cl, Bn, Hn. . . . Costallat(1853); IMC, AMP
SPOHR   Octet--E, Op 32.  Cl, 2Hn, Vl, 2Va, Vc, Cb.  . . . Eulenberg(1888); Peters
THIERIOT   Octet--Bb, Op 62.  With Cl, Bn, Hn. . . . . . Peters(1893)


## 4 Winds, with StrQuar unless otherwise given.

BACH, J. S.  Musical Offering.  Fl, Ob, EH, Bn.  Ed: H. David. . . . . . . . . . . . . GSch
HOFMANN   Octet--F, Op 80.  Fl, Cl, Bn, Hn. . . . . . . . . . . B&H(1880); AMP
MOZART   Serenade #2--F, K 101 (1776).  2Ob, 2Hn, 2Vl, Vc, Cb. . . . . B&H; AMP
PETERS   Nocturne--F.  Ob, Cl, Bn, Hn. . . . . . . . . . . . . . . UE(1918); Peters
PIERNE, GABR.  Petite Gavotte.  Fl, Ob, Cl, Hn. . . . . . . . . . Spratt, MBaron
PURCELL   Lament from "Dido & Aeneas".  Arr: WWQuar by Finney. . . Witmark; MPHC
REICHA   Octet--Eb, Op 96.  Ob, Cl, Bn, Hn. . . . . . . . . . . . . . . . . .
WALTER, AUG.  Octet--Bb, Op 7.  Ob, Cl, Bn, Hn, Vl, Va, Vc, Cb.  . . . . Kistner(1850)


## 8 Woodwinds: Fl, Ob, 2 Cl, 2 Bn, 2 Hn

GOUVY   Octet--Eb, Op 71. . . . . . . . . . . . . . Kistner(1882); Andraud
LACHNER   Octet--Bb, Op 156. . . . . . . . . . . . Kistner(1872)
REINECKE   Octet--Bb, Op 216. . . . . . . . . . . . Kistner(1892); Andraud
SAINT-SAENS   "Album Leaves" for Pf 4 hds., Op 81.  Arr: Taffanel . . . Durand; E-V


## 8 Woodwinds: 2 Ob, 2 Cl, 2 Bn, 2 Hn

BEETHOVEN   Octet--Eb, Op 103 (c1794).  . . . . . . . B&H(1863); AMP, IMC
        Rondino--Eb, Op"146"(1790-92) . . . . . . B&H(1864); AMP
        Serenade--Eb, [Op ?] . . . . . . . . . . Broude
HAYDN   Octet--F.  Ed: Grutzmacher. . . . . . . . . . Kahnt(1901); Marks, IMC
        Divertimento, Feldpartita--Bb.  Ed: Geiringer. . . F. Schuberth, jr(1932)
MOZART   Divertimento--Eb, K 196e[Anh. 226](1775).. Ozalid pts: Christlieb, c/o W. W. Mag.
        Divertimento--Bb, K 196f[Anh. 227] (1775). .Ozalid pts: Christlieb, c/o W. W. Mag.
        Serenade #11--Eb, K 375 (1782 version).  Arr: Mozart . . . B&H; Broude
        Serenade #12--c mi, K 388 (1782). . . . . . . Andre(1875); Broude
REUSS   Octet--B, Op 37. . . . . . . . . . . . . . . Zimmerman(1920); Andraud

8 Woodwinds:  2 Ob, 2 Cl, 2 Bn, 2 Hn  cont.

SCHUBERT, FR.   Minuet & Finale of an Octet--F (1813) . . . . . . .   B&H(1889); A
STRANENSKY   Parthia--F.   Ed: Schultz, in Erbe dt. Musik . . . . .   Nagel


8 Woodwinds:  Misc.

CAMPBELL-WATSON   Divertimento.   Fl, Ob, 2Cl, Bn, BsCl, 2Hn. . . .   Witmark,
DALLEY   Reverie.   2Fl, Ob, 2Cl, 2Bn, Hn. . . . . . . . . . . . .   Witmark; Mr.
DUBOIS   1st Suite.   2Fl, Ob, 2Cl, 2Bn, Hn. . . . . . . . . .   Heugel(1898); Andraud
         2nd Suite . . . ditto . . . . . . . . . . . . . . .   Leduc(1898); MBaron
         In the Garden.   Fl&Picc, Fl, Ob, [2?]Bn, Hn. . . . . . . . . . .   Andraud
KLING   Spring Poetry.   Fl, 2Ob, 2Cl, 2Bn, Hn. . . . . . . . . . . . .   Andraud
LAZZARI   Octet--F, Op 20 (1890).   Fl, Ob, EH, Cl, 2Bn, 2Hn. .   Evette & S(1920); Andraud
LULLY   Menuet du Bourgeois Gentilhomme.   Arr: EbCl, 4Cl, 2Bn, CBn. . . . .   Andraud
PETYREK   Divertimento--Bb (1923).   Fl&Picc, Fl, Ob, Cl, 2Bn, 2Hn. . . . . .   Andraud
POLDOWSKI   Octet.   2Fl, Ob, Ob d'amour, EH, Cl, BassetHn, BsCl. . . . . . . . .
SCARLATTI, (?).   Allegro from 8th Suite--Bb.   Arr: Fl, 2Ob, 2Cl, 2Bn, Hn. . . .   Andraud
TANSMAN   Four Impressions for Octet.   Double WWQuar. . . . . . . . . .   Leeds
WEINGARTNER   Octet--G, Op 73.   Arr: 2Fl, Ob, Cl, 2Bn, 2Hn by ? . . . . . .   Andraud


8 Brass:  Misc.

CORELLI   Concerto Grosso, Op 6#11.   Arr: 4Ct, Hn, 2Bar, Tuba by King. .   Mus f Brass
ELGAR   Th. from "Pomp & Circumstance #1".   Arr: 4Tt, 3Tb, Tb(Tuba). .   Boosey
GABRIELI   Sonata Pian e Forte.   Arr: 2Ct, 2Hn, 3Tb, Tuba(BsTb) by Harvey . . .   E-V
           ditto . . . . .   Arr: 2Ct, Hn, 3Tb, Bar, Tuba . . . . .   Mus f Brass
           Canzon septimi toni #2.   Ed: 4Ct, 2Hn(Tb), 2Bar (2 equal choirs),
                                                  by King . . . .   Mus f Brass
           Canzon noni toni.   Ed: 4Ct, 2Hn(Tb), 2Bar  (2 equal choirs),
                                                  by King . . . .   Mus f Brass
LASSUS   Providebam Dominum.   Ed: 4Ct, Ct(Hn), Tb, Bar, Tuba by King. .   Mus f Brass


Misc. including Perc.

ALTENBURG   Concerto for Clarini & Tymp.   Arr: 5Ct, 2Ct(Hn), Tymp
                                                  by King . . . . . .   Mus f Brass
BACH, K. P. E.   6 Marches.   2Ob, 2Cl, Bn, 2Hn, Perc. . . . . . . . . . .   Marks
MOZART   Organ [i. e. Church] Sonatas #12, 14[--G, C; K 274, 336 (1777, 1780)]
                        Arr: 2Ob, 2Tt, 2Vl, Vc, Tymp by ? . . . . . . . . .   Merc
SCHMID   Turm-musik, Op 105.   Arr: 6Tt, 2Perc. . . . . . . . . . . . . .   B&H
SCHMIDT, G. FR.   Heldenehrung.   2Tt, 3Tb, Tuba, 2Perc. . . . . . . . .   B&H(1940)


8 Misc. Insts.

CODIVILLA   Ottetto--Eb.   WWQuar, Ct, 2Hn, Tb. . . . . . . . . . . .   Pizzi(1919)
GAL   Divertimento--Op 22.   Fl, Ob, 2Cl, Bn, 2Hn, Tt. . . . . . . . . .   Leuckart(1925)
GRAINGER   My Robin is to the Greenwood Gone.   Fl, EH, 6Str.
                  (This is the orig. orchestration). . . . . . .   Schott(London, 1916)
KAUN, HUGO   Octet, Op 26[?].   For winds. . . . . . . . . . . . . . .
PASCAL   Octet.   2Fl, Ob, Cl, 2Bn, Hn, Tt. . . . . . . . . . . .   Durand; E-V

8 Misc. Insts.  cont.

PAZ   Octet (1930).  Winds. . . . . . . . . . . . . . . . . . . . .
RIISAGER   Sinfonietta.   Fl, Cl, 2Bn, 2Tt, 2Tb. . . . . . . . . Andraud
STRAVINSKY   Octet (1923).   Fl, Cl, 2Bn, 2Tt, 2Tb. . . . . . . Russ. M-V(1924); Boosey
VARESE   Octandre.   WWQuint, Tt, Tb, Cb. . . . . . . . . . . Curwen(1924)
WAGENAAR   Concertino for 8 Insts. (1942).   WWQuint, Vl, Va, Vc. . . . . CFisch
WAILLY   Octet.   Fl, Ob, 2Cl, 2Bn, Hn, Tt.   . . . . . . . . . Rouart 2nd mvt. only
WEISSE   Octet (1929).   Strs & Winds. . . . . . . . . . . . . . . . . .
WELLESZ   Octet.   3 W. W. & 5 Str. . . . . . . . . . . Lengnick(London); Mills
WILDER   Walking Home in Spring;  Such a Tender Night;  She'll Be Seven
          in May;  Seldom the Sun;  Neurotic Goldfish;  A Debutante's
          Diary.   All Mixed Wind Octets. . . . . . . . . . . . Andraud


## 8 INSTS. : including Pf(Keyboard, etc. )

### 3 Insts. , with StrQuar & Pf

DUPONT   Octet.   Cl, Bn, Hn. . . . . . . . . . . . . . Hamelle(1935)
TAILLEFERRE   Image, prelude (1918).   Fl, Cl, Celeste. . . . Chester; Andraud
WEINGARTNER   Octet--G, Op 73.   Cl, Bn, Hn. . . . . . . Birnbach(1915)


### 3 Insts. , with Vl, Va, Vc, Cb, Pf

DOLMETSCH   Octuor--f mi, Op 27.   Ob(Fl), Cl, Hn. . . . . . Costallat(1858)
RIES   Octet--Ab, Op 128 (1818).   Cl, Bn, Hn. . . . . . . . Kistner
RUBINSTEIN   Octet--D, Op 9.   Fl, Cl, Hn. . . . . . . . . Hamelle(1856), Peters


### 2 Insts. , with StrQuint & Pf(Hp)

ABEL   Concerto for Pf--Eb.   2Fl; Pf is solo. . . . . . . . Peters
ARRIAGA y BALZOLA   Octeto.   Tt, Guitar. . . . . . Comision permanente Arriaga(1929)
LOEFFLER   Octet (1897).   2Cl; uses Hp. . . . . . . . . . . . . . . . .
ZICH   Octet.   Hn, Bn. . . . . . . . . . . . . . . . . Hudebni Matice(c1930)


### Misc. , including Pf(Hp)

BAX   Octet (1934).   Hn, StrSextet, Pf. . . . . . . . . . . . . .
      Concerto (1936).   Bn, StrSextet, Hp. . . . . . . . . . . . .
BAZELAIRE   Greek Suite.   2Fl, Ob, Vl, Va, 2Vc, Hp(Pf). . . . Schneider (1927); Andraud
GREEN   3 Pcs. for a Concert.   Fl, 2Cl, 2Tt, Tb, Pf, Perc. . . . . . . . . . . Marks
HANDEL   Concerti #5, 6--d mi, D; from 6 Concerti Op 3.
          2Ob Primo, 2Vl, Va, Vc, Continuo(Pf&Vc).   Werke XXI  . . B&H(1858)
          Concerto Grosso #10.   Ob, StrQuint, 2Pf. . . . . . . . . B-N
JUON   Octet--Bb, Op 27a.   Ob, Cl, Bn, Hn, Vl, Va, Vc, Pf. . . . Lienau(1907); ECSch
LIADOV   Musical Snuff Box, Op 32.   Picc, 2Fl, 3Cl, Hp, Bells. . Belaiev; AMP
LOUIS FERDINAND   Octet--f mi, Op 12.   Cl, 2Hn, 2Vl, 2Vc, Pf. . . . . . . . . B&H

# NINE INSTRUMENTS

## 9 INSTS.

### 4 Woodwinds:  with StrQuint

DUBOIS  Nonet.  WWQuar. . . . . . . . . . . . . . . . . Heugel(1926); Andraud
HESELTINE   An Old Song.  Fl, Ob, Cl, Hn. . . . . . . . . . . . . . .
KORNAUTH   Kammermusik--f mi, Op 31.  Fl, Ob, Cl, Hn. . . . Doblinger(1926); Andraud
KRENEK  Symphonic music, Op 11 (1922).  WWQuar. . . . . . UE(1923)
        Symphonic Music Divertimento, Op 23.  Fl, Cl, Hn, Bn. . . . . . . . Andraud
MOLBE  Tanzweisen, Op 26.  Ob, Cl, Bn, Hn.  . . . . . . . . Hofmeister(1896)
      Nonet--Eb, Op 61.  EH, Cl, Bn, Hn.  . . . . . . . Hofmeister(1897)
      Intermezzo--g mi, Op 81.  Ob, Cl, Bn, Hn. . . . . . . Hofmeister(1900)
      Scherzo; Andante pensieroso--F, G; Op 83, 84.  Ob, Cl, Bn, Hn. . Hofmeister(c1900)
      Tanzweisen--Eb, Op 89.  Ob, Cl, Bn, Hn.  . . . . . . . . . Hofmeister(c1900)
NAUMANN, ERNST  Serenade--A, Op 10.  Fl, Ob, Bn, Hn. . . . Simrock(1872); AMP
NAUMANN, R.  Kammermusik, Op 31.  Fl, Ob, Cl, Hn.  . . . . Doblinger(1926)


### 5 Woodwinds:  WWQuint, with Vl, Va, Vc, Cb  unless otherwise given.

HARSANYI   Nonet.  With StrQuar instead. . . . . . . . . . Lemoine(1930)
MOSER, FR. J.   Sinfonie for 9 Solo Insts. --F, Op 40. . . . . . Doblinger(1924); Andraud
ONSLOW  Nonet--a mi, Op 77.  . . . . . . . . . . . . . Joubert(1851), Kistner
RHEINBERGER  Nonet--Eb, Op 139. . . . . . . . . . . . Kistner & S(1885)
RIDKY  Nonett, Op 32. . . . . . . . . . . . . . . . . . Sadlo(1941)
SAMAZEUILH  Divertissement et musette--g mi.  With StrQuar. . . . Durand(1902)
SCHOECK  Serenade, Op 1.  With StrQuar. . . . . . . . . . Hug(1907)
SPOHR  Nonet--F, Op 31. . . . . . . . . . . . . . . . Haslinger(1876); Peters


### 9 Woodwinds:  2 Fl, Ob, 2 Cl, 2 Bn, 2 Hn

SAINT-SAENS  Deuxieme Suite [for Orch?].  Arr. ? . . . . . B-N
SCHRECK  Divertimento--e mi, Op 40.  Fl, Fl&Picc. . . . . . B&H(1905); AMP


### 9 Woodwinds:  Fl, 2 Ob, 2 Cl, 2 Bn, 2 Hn

BONVIN  Romanze, Op 19a. . . . . . . . . . . . . . . . B&H
      Melodie.  . . . . . . . . . . . . . . . . . . . . B&H
BRÄUTIGAM   Kleine Jagdmusik. . . . . . . . . . . . . B&H (1939)
GOOSENS[?]  Petite Symphonie. . . . . . . . . . . . . Costallat
GOUNOD  Petite Symphonie--Bb. . . . . . . . . . . . . Costallat(1904); MBaron
GOUVY  Petite Suite Gauloise, Op 90. . . . . . . . . . . UE(1900); Peters
LANGE, G. FR.  Nonet--F. . . . . . . . . . . . . . . . Erdmann(1879)
PARRY  Nonet--Bb, Op 70 (1877).  1 Ob is on EH. . . . . . . . . . .

## 9 Woodwinds:  2 Fl, 2 Ob, 2 Cl, 2 Bn, Hn

PISTON    Divertimento for 9 Insts (1946).  . . . . . . . . . .  Broadcast; AMP
STÜRMER    Suite--g mi, Op 9.  . . . . . . . . . . . . . .  Schott(1923); AMP


## 9 Woodwinds:  Misc.

BIZET    Minuet from "l'Arlesienne Suite #1".
        Arr: Fl, Ob, EbCl, 2Cl, AltCl, BsCl, BarSx, Hn by Cheyette-Roberts.  .  CFisch
BURGMEIN    Noel! Noel!  Picc, Fl,2Ob, EH, 2Cl, 2Bn.  Arr: Mugnone .  . B&H[Boosey?]
CIANCHI    Nonetto.  2Ob, 2Cl, 2Bn, CBn, 2Hn. . . . . . . . .  Paoletti(Florence, 1868)
MARTEAU, H.    Serenade--D, Op 22.  2Fl, 2Ob, 2Cl, BsCl, 2Bn.  . .  Steingräber(1922)


## 9 Winds:  Misc.

GOOSENS    Phantasy Nonet, Op 40 (1924).  Fl, Ob, 2Cl, 2Bn, 2Hn, Tt.  . . . Curwen(1925)
SCHEIN    Dances from Banquetto Musicale.  9 Winds . . . . . . .  McG & M
SCHUBERT, FR.    Eine Kleine Trauermusik--Eb (1812).
        2Cl, 2Bn, CBn, 2Hn, 2Tb. . . . . . . . . .  B&H(1889); AMP
SETACCIOLI    Nonet.   Wind insts. . . . . . . . . . . . . . . . . . . . . .


## 8 Insts. & Perc

ADLER    Praeludium.  2Ct, 2Hn, 2Tb, Bar, Tuba, Tymp.  . . . . . . .  Mus f Brass
CHEMIN-PETIT    Kleine Suite nach puppenspiel Dr. Faust.
        Ob, Cl, Bn, StrQuint, Perc.  . . . . . .  Lienau(1940)
NIELSEN, (L. ?)  Bagpipe, Op 30.  2Fl, 2Ob, 2Cl, 2Bn, Perc. . . . . .  Andraud
WEINBERGER    Concerto for Tymp.   Tymp, 4Tt, 4Tb.  . . . . . . .  AMP


## 9 Misc. Insts.

BRUN    Passacaille, Op 25.  2Fl, Ob, 2Cl, Bn, 2Hn, Cb. . . . . . . . .  Andraud
CATURLA    Nonet #10 . . . . . . . . . . . . . . . .  New Music Orch. Ser. ; Andraud
MERIKANTO    Concert.   Vl, Cl, Hn, StrSextet.  . . . . . . . . . .  Schott(1925); AMP
PLEYEL    Serenade.   8Winds, Cb.  . . . . . . . . . . . . .  Rudall & Carte
SALVIUCCI    Serenata.   WWQuar, Tt, StrQuar. . . . . . . . . .  Ricordi(1927)
SILAS    Nonet.   Strs & Winds. . . . . . . . . . . . . . . . . . . .


## 9 INSTS.:   including Pf(Keyboard, etc. )

## 3 Winds:  with StrQuint & Pf(Hp)

BAX    Nonet.   Fl, Ob, Cl; uses Hp. . . . . . . . . . . . . .  Murdoch(1932)
GILCHRIST    Nonet.   Fl, Cl, Hn. . . . . . . . . . . . . . . . . . .

## 4 Winds:  with StrQuar & Pf(Hp)

GIVOTOV    Fragments for Nonetto, Op 2.   Fl, Cl, Bn, Tt . . . . . . . . . . . UE(1930)
MILHAUD    Symph. #1, "Printemps"(1917).   Picc, Fl, Cl, Ob; uses Hp. . . . UE(1922); Merc
STÖHR    Kammersymphonie--F, Op 32.   Ob, Cl, Bn, Hn; uses Hp. . . . . . Kahnt(1921)
WEBERN    Sinfonie, Op 21.   Cl, BsCl, 2Hn; uses Hp. . . . . . . . . . UE(1930)


## Misc.

BERTINI    Nonet--D, Op 107.   Fl, Ob, Bn, Hn, Tt, Va, Vc, Cb, Pf. . . . . Lemoine
BUMCKE    Der Spaziergang, Op 22.   WWQuint, EH, AltCl, [BsCl?], Hp. .  Ries & Erler(1906)
BURGMEIN    O Mama Cara, Preghiera.   2Fl, 2Ob, 2Cl, Bn, Hn, Hp.
                                     Arr:   Mugnone.  . . .   B&H[Boosey?]
COLERIDGE-TAYLOR    Nonet--f mi, Op 2.   W. W. , Strs, Pf. . . . . . . . . . . . .
FICHER    From ballet Los Invitados, Op 26 (1933).
                     FL, Cl, AltSx, TenSx, 2Tt, Tb, Perc. Pf. . . . . . . . . . . .
McPHEE    Concerto.   Wind Octet, Pf. . . . . . . . . . . . . . NME IV#2(1930)
SHEBERBACKER    Nonet, Op 10.   Winds, Strs, Pf. . . . . . . . . . UE

# TEN INSTRUMENTS

### 4 Woodwinds: with 2 Vl, 2 Va, Vc, Cb unless otherwise given.

| | | |
|---|---|---|
| HAYDN | Notturno #1--C. Fl, Ob, 2Hn. Ed: Schmid. . . . . | Musikw. V(1937) |
| | Notturno #2--C[F?]. 2Fl, 2Hn. Ed: Schmid. . . . | Musikw. V(1937) |
| | ditto --F. Fl, Ob, 2Hn. . . . . . . . . . | Hohler & Schäfler(Karlsbad) |
| | Nottorno #5--C. Fl, Ob, 2Hn. Ed: Geiringer. . . . | UE(1931) |
| | Partita--F. Fl, Ob, 2Hn. Ed: Geiringer. . . . . . | UE(1932) |
| MOLBE | Dixtet--c mi, Op 21. 3Vl, Va, Vc, Cb, Cl, EH, Bn, Hn. . | Hofmeister(1896) |

### 5 Woodwinds: WWQuint, StrQuint unless otherwise given.

| | | |
|---|---|---|
| DUBOIS | Dixtuor--d mi. Cl is EbCl. . . . . . . . . . . | Heugel(1909); Andraud |
| FLEGIER | Dixtuor--f mi. . . . . . . . . . . . . . . . | Lemoine(c1900) |
| KLINGLER | Variationem--A. . . . . . . . . . . . . . | Author publ. (Berlin, 1938) |
| LALO | Aubade, Morning Serenade (1871). . . . . . . . . | Heugel |
| MOOR | Suite--A, Op 103. . . . . . . . . . . . . . | Salabert(1913); Andraud |
| PIERNE, GABR. | March of Little Fauns. . . . . . . . . . | Andraud |
| REICHA | Dixtet. 5 W. W. , 5Str. . . . . . . . . . . . . . . | |
| STRIEGLER | Kammer-sinfonie, Op 14. Playable StrQuint or Quar. . . | Junne(1912) |

### 10 Woodwinds: Double WWQuint

| | | |
|---|---|---|
| BERNARD, E. | Divertissement--F, Op 36. . . . . . . . . . | Durand(1890); E-V |
| BIRD | Pavane. . . . . . . . . . . . . . . . . . . | Andraud |
| BLATTNER | 2 American Sketches. . . . . . . . . . . . | Witmark; MPHC |
| CAPLET | Suite Persane (1900). . . . . . . . . . . . | Ms at Curtis |
| CASADESUS | London Sketches. . . . . . . . . . . . | Deisz & Co. (1916); MBaron |
| ENESCO | Dixtet--D, Op 14. 1 Ob is on EH. . . . . . . . . | Ms at Curtis |
| JADASSOHN | Serenade, Op 104c. . . . . . . . . . . . . | Andraud |
| MELLIN | Minuet Badin. . . . . . . . . . . . . . | Evette |
| RAFF | Sinfonietta--F, Op 188. . . . . . . . . . . . | Kistner(1876) |
| SPORCK | Landscapes Normandy. . . . . . . . . . . . | Andraud |
| TANEIEV | Andante. Arr: Lamm. . . . . . . . . . . . . . | Leeds |

### 10 Woodwinds: Misc.

| | | |
|---|---|---|
| MILHAUD | Symph. #5. Picc, Fl, Ob, EH, Cl, BsCl, 2Bn, 2Hn. . . . . . . | UE(1922) |
| MOZART | Divertimento #3--Eb, K 166 (1773). 2Ob, 2EH, 2Cl, 2Bn, 2Hn... | B&H(1879); AMP |
| | Divertimento #4--Bb, K 186 (1773). 2Ob, 2EH, 2Cl, 2Bn, 2Hn... | B&H(1879); AMP |
| SCHMITT | Lied & Scherzo, Op 54 (1910). | |
| | Solo Hn, Fl&Picc, Fl, Ob, EH, 2Cl, Hn, 2Bn . . . . . | Durand; E-V |

## 10 Brass:  Misc.

ARNELL   Ceremonial & Flourish.  3Tt, 4Hn, 3Tb. . . . . . . .   AMP
BONELLI   Toccata.   2Ct, 2Hn(Ct), 2Tb, 2Bar, 2Tuba (2 equal choirs).
                                   Ed:  King. . . . . .   Mus f Brass
GABRIELI   Canzon Septimi Toni.   4Tt, 2Hn, 4Tb (2 equal choirs) . . . MBaron
KING   7 Conversation Pcs.   4Ct, 3Tb, 2Bar, Tuba. . . . . . . . . . Mus f Brass
WEBER, C. M.   Marcia Vivace--D.   10 Tt. . . . . . . . . . . . . . . . . .

## Misc.

BRESGEN   Bläsermusik, Op 17.   10 Insts. . . . . . . . . . . . Vieweg(1937)   91, 118,
ENESCO   Intermezzo for 10 Wind Insts, [Op 12?], . . . . . . . . . . . . . . . .
HARTMANN   Serenade--Bb, Op 43.   Fl, Ob, 2Cl, 2Bn, 2Hn, Vc, Cb. . . Ries & E(1890)
RIETI   Madrigal in 4 Pts.   [4 mvts.]. . . . . . . . . . . . . . Andraud

## 10 INSTS. :  including Pf(Keyboard, etc. )

## 4 Winds:  with StrQuint & Pf(Hp)

LOUIS FERDINAND   Rondo--Bb, Op 9.   Fl, Cl, 2Hn. . . . . . . . . . . . . . . . . B&H
MOLBE   Hymne de printemps, Op 31.   EH, Cl, Bn, Hn; uses Hp. . . . . . . . . . .
          7 Dixtets--Eb, F, Bb, Ab, C, Bb, C; Op 91, 104, 109, 113, 118, 124, 129.
                    EH, Cl, Bn, Hn; uses Hp. . . . . . . . . . . . Hofmeister(1901-10)
          2 Dixtets--Bb, F; Op 110, 111.   EH, Cl, Bn, Hn; uses Hp. . . . . . . . . . . .
          Grüne Klänge.   EH, Cl, Bn, Hn; uses Hp. . . . . . . . . Hofmeister(1912)

## 5 Winds:  with StrQuar & Hp

IBERT   Capriccio.   WWQuar, Tt. . . . . . . . . . . . . . . . Leduc(1939); MBaron
PITTALUGA   Petite Suite.   Fl, Cl, Bn, Tt, Tb. . . . . . . . . . Spratt, MBaron

## Misc.

LEVIDIS   Divertimento (1927).   Solo EH, StrQuint, 2Hp, Celeste, Perc. . . . . . . . . . . . . .

# ELEVEN INSTRUMENTS

6 Winds: with StrQuint

GRIMM, H.   Byzantine Suite.   WWQuint, Tt. . . . . . . . . . .   Andraud


11 Winds

PARRIS   4 Rhapsodies for Brass Ens.   3Tt, 4Hn, 3Tb, Tuba.   . . .   E-V
PAZ   Var. for 11 Wind Insts. (1928-29). . . . . . . . . . . . . . . .
ROY   Tripartita, Op 5.   3Ct, 2Hn, 3Tb, 2Bar, Tuba. . . . . . . . .   Mus f Brass
SCARLATTI, (A. ?) Pastoral & Capriccio.   Double WWQuint, Tt.
                                Arr: Hasselmans. . . . . . . .   Andraud


Misc.

BRAUER   Pan, Suite.   10 Winds, Cb. . . . . . . . . . . . . . . . .   B&H(1934)
MALIPIERO   Ricercari (1925).   Fl&Picc, Ob, Cl, Bn, Hn, 4Va, Vc, Cb. . .   UE(1926); Peters
            Ritrovari (1926).   Fl&Picc, Ob, Cl, Bn, Hn, 4Va, Vc, Cb. . .   UE(1927); Peters
MOZART   Divertimento #5--C, K 187 (1773).   2Fl, 5Tt, 4Dr. . . . . .   B&H(1880); AMP
         Divertimento #6--C, K 188 (1773).   2Fl, 5Tt, 4Dr. . . . . .   B&H(1880); AMP


11 INSTS. : including Pf(Keyboard, etc. )

WWQuint, StrQuint, Pf(Hp)

BLOCH   4 Episodes (1926). . . . . . . . . . . . . . . . . .   Birchard
LENDVAI   Kammersuite, Op 32.   Uses Hp. . . . . . . . . . . . .   Rahter(1923)
SEKLES   Serenade--Eb, Op 14.   Uses Hp. . . . . . . . . . . . .   Rahter(1907)
WOLF-FERRARI   Chamber Symphony--Bb, Op 8. . . . . . . . .   Rahter(1903)


Misc.

CATURLA   Bembe.   Fl, Ob&EH, 2Cl, Bn, StrQuar, Perc, Pf. . . . . . . . . . .   Senart
          ditto . . Fl, Ob&EH, 2Cl, Bn, Tt, 2Hn, Tb, Perc, Pf. . . . . . . . . .   Senart
COSSART   Suite--F, Op 19.   Double WWQuint, Hp. . . . . . .   Heinrichshofen(1908)
EICHHEIM   Oriental Impressions (1921).   Fl, Ob, 4Vl, Va, Hp, Pf, Bells, Perc. . . . GSch
RUYNEMAN   Hieroglyphs.   3Fl, Tt, 2Mandolin, 2Guitar, Pf, Celeste, CupBells. . . . Chester
STRAVINSKY   Ragtime for 11 Insts. (1918).
              Fl, Cl, Hn, Ct, Tb, 2Vl, Va, Cb, Cymbalum, Perc. . . . . . . Chester
TOMASI   Jeux de Geishas.   5Winds, StrQuar, Hp(Pf), Perc. . . . . . . . . . Durand(1939)

# TWELVE INSTRUMENTS

## 12 INSTS

### Woodwinds

PERILHOU    Divertissement (1904).   Double WWQuar, 4Hn. . . . .. Heugel; Andraud

### Brass

ADLER   Divertimento.   3Ct, 3Hn, 3Tb, 2Bar, Tuba. . . . . . . . Mus f Brass
GABRIELI    Sonata octavi toni.   2 choirs,   I: 2Ct, 2Tb, Bar, Tuba
                                      II: 2Ct, 2Tb(Hn), Bar, Tuba
              Ed: King. . . . . . . . . . . . . . . . . Mus f Brass

### Brass & Tymp

ADLER   Concert Piece.   3Ct, 2Hn, 3Tb, 2Bar, Tuba, Tymp. . . . . . . Mus f Brass
BEADELL   Intro. & Allegro.   3Ct, 3Hn, 3Tb, Bar, Tuba, Tymp. . . . . . Mus f Brass
HARTMEYER   Negev, a Tone Poem.   3Ct, 3Hn, 3Tb, Bar, Tuba, Tymp . . Mus f Brass
LIADOV   No. 1, 2, 4* of "Slavlania" (1890).   3Tt, 4Hn, 3Tb, Tymp. . . . Belaiev
MARKS   Intro. & Passacaglia (1949).   3Ct, 3Hn, 3Tb, Bar, Tuba, Tymp . . Mus f Brass
REYNOLDS   Th. & Var. (1950).   3Ct, 3Hn, 3Tb, Bar, Tuba, Tymp. . . . . Mus f Brass

### Misc.

BUSCH, (A. ?)   Divertimento.   WWQuar, 2Hn, Tt, StrQuar, Tymp. . Andraud
DVORAK   March from Serenade, Op 44.
                      Arr: 2Ob, 2Cl, 2Bn, CBn, 3Hn, Vc, Cb. . . . Marks
HANDEL   Fireworks Music, 2 parts.   I: 3Ob, 2Bn, 3Hn, 3Tt, Tymp.
                                    II: 2Ob, Bn, 3Hn, 3Tt, Tymp.
              (Alternate and added insts. possible). . . . Marks
STRAVINSKY   Song of Hauleurs on the Volga.
                      Picc, Fl, Ob, Cl, Bn, 2Hn, 3Tt, Tuba, Perc. . . Chester; Andraud

### 12 INSTS. : including Pf(Keyboard, etc. )

CATURLA   Tres Danza Cubanas.
              Fl&Picc, Ob&EH, Cl, BsCl, Bn, 2Hn, Tt, Tb, Tuba, Perc. Pf. . . E-V
HOLBROOKE   Serenade, Op 61b.   5AltSx, Ob, EH, Cl, 2Saxhorn, Va, Hp. . . . . Andraud
LELEU   Suite Symphonic.   2Fl&Picc, Ob, EH, Cl, Bn, Hn, 2Tt, Tb, Pf, Perc. . . . Leduc

---

*No. 3 & 5 are by Glazounov.

# MISCELLANEOUS

## LARGER GROUPS & MISC.

_____ Master W. W. Ens. Series.   Various combinations of:
    Fl, Ob, Cl, AltCl, BsCl, Bn, AltSx, TenSx, BarSx, Hn.
     Ed: Cheyette, Roberts. . . . . . . . . . . . . . CFisch
BECKHELM   Tragic March.   4Ct, 4Hn, 3Tb, Bar, Tuba, Tymp, Perc. . . Mus f Brass
BERG   Chamber Concerto (1923-25).   Pf, Vl, 13 Winds. . . . . . . . . . .
BONNEAU   Fanfare,   3Tt, 3Hn, 2Tb, Tuba, 4Tymp. . . . . . . . . . Andraud
BRADLEY   The Deep Quarry.   Woodwinds. . . . . . . . . . . . NME XXI#4(1948)
    Honeysuckle & Clover.   Brass choir. . . . . . . . . . NME XXI#4(1948)
DeMEESTER   Divertissement.   For brasses. . . . . . . . . . . . . . . . . .
EWALD   Quint--b flat mi, Op 5.   Arr: Brass choir of 2Ct, Hn, Tb, Bar, Tuba;
     by King. . . . . . . . . . . . . Mus f Brass
FRIED   Adagio & Scherzo, Op 2.   3Fl&Picc, 3Ob, 3Cl, 3Bn, 3Hn, 2Hp, Tymp. . . . . . B&H
GABRIELI   Canzon duodecimi toni.   4Ct, 2Hn, 2Tb, 2Bar, 2Tuba (in 2
     equal choirs); Organ optional.   Ed: King. . . . . . Mus f Brass
    Canzon quarti toni.   3 choirs as follows,
      I: Ct, Ct(Hn), Tb, Bar, Tuba
      II: 4Tb, Tuba
      III: Ct, Ct(Hn), 2Bar, Tuba. . . . . . . . Mus f Brass
GILSON   Norwegian Melody; Humoresques.   W. W. , Hns. . . . . . . . . . .
GOLDMAN   Hymn for Brass Choir (1939).   16 insts. . . . . . . . . NME XV#1(1941)
GRABNER   Perkeo.   Fl&Picc, Fl, 2Ob, 2Cl, 3Bn, 4Hn, Dr. . . . . . Kahnt
GRAINGER   Ye Banks & Braie o'Bonnie Doon (1932).
    Picc, WWQuint, EH, AltCl, BsCl, AltSx, TenSx, BarSx, BsSx.
    (Playable by various combinations of these). . . . . . GSch
HAHN   Ball of Beatrice d'Este.   2Fl, Ob, 2Cl, 2Bn, 2Hn, Tt, 2Hp, Pf, StrQuar.
        . . . . . Heugel; MBaron
HANDEL 6 Concerti--Bb, Bb, G, F, d, D; Op3.
    #1:   2Vl, 2Ob, 2Fl, 2Va, 2Bn, Continuo.
    #2:   2Vl Conc. , 2Vl Rip. , 2Ob, Va, 2Vc, Continuo.
    #3:   Vl Conc. , 2Vl Rip. , Fl(Ob), Va, Continuo incl. Vc.
    #4:   2Vl, 2Ob, Va, Bn, Continuo.
    #5:   2Ob, Primo, 2Vl, Va, Vc, Continuo
    #6:   ditto . . . . . . . . , Organo. . in Werke XXI. . B&H(1858)
   Concerto Grosso--C (1736).   2Ob, {Conc: 2Vl, Vc} Va, Continuo.
           {Rip: 2Vl}
       . . . in Werke XXI. . B&H(1858)
HERBERIGS   Concert champetre.   Winds. . . . . . . . . . . . . . . . . . . . .
HINDEMITH   Chamber Music #2, Op 36#1.
    Pf, Fl, Ob, Cl, Bn, BsCl, Tt, Hn, Tb, Vl, Va, Vc, Cb. . . Andraud
LAMPE   Serenade, Op 7.   2Fl, 2Ob, EH, 2Cl, BsCl, 2Bn, CBn, 4Hn. . . . Simrock
McKAY   Bravura Prelude.   4Tt, 4Hn, 4Tb, 2Bar, Tuba. . . . . . . AMP
MENDELSSOHN, A. L.   Suite.   Fl&Picc, Fl, 2Ob, 2Cl, 2Bn, 2Hn, 2Tt, 3Tb,
      , Tymp, Triangle, Tamb. . . . . . . . Leuckart
MOSER, F. J.   Serenade, Op 35 (1921).   Fl&Picc, Fl, 3Ob, 3Cl, 3Bn, 4Hn. . . . . UE

MOZART    Serenade #10--Bb,  K 361 (1780).
                        2Ob, 2Cl, 2BassetHn, 2Bn, 4Hn, Cb(CBn) . . . . B&H(1880); AMP
OLDBERG  Quintet, Op 18.  W. W. , Pf. . . . . . . . . . . . . . . . . . .
PETRIDIS  Concerto Grosso (1929).  Winds.  . . . . . . . . . . . . . . . . .
PETYREK  Arabische Suite (1924).
                Fl&Picc, Fl, Ob, 2Cl, 2Bn, 2Hn, Tb, Cb, Tymp, Perc, Hp. . . UE
READ  Sound Piece, Op 82.  4Tt, 4Hn, 3Tb, Bar, Tuba, Tymp, Perc. . . . . Mus f Brass
REZNICEK  Traumspiel.  Fl&Picc, Ob&EH, Cl, BsCl, Bn, Hn, Tt, Vl, Va,
                Vc, a 5 string Cb, Perc, Hp, Celeste(Pf). . . . Simrock
RIEGGER  Music for Brass Choir, Op 45 (1948-49).
                10Tt, 8Hn, 10Tb, 2Tuba, Perc. . . . . . . . Merrymount; Merc
SCHISKE  Trompetermusik, Op 13.  10Tt, 8Tb, 2Tuba, Perc. . . . . . . . . . . . . .
SCHÖNBERG  Chamber Symphony--E, Op 9 (1913).
         Fl, Ob, EH, Cl in D, Cl in A, BsCl, Bn, CBn, 2Hn, StrQuar.
         Ed. and simplified by Webern. . . . . . . . . . . UE(1906)
SALMHOFER  Kammersuite, Op 19.  Fl&Picc, 2Ob, Cl, Cl&BsCl, 2Bn, 2Hn,
                Hp, StrQuint. . . . . . . . . . . UE
STANFORD  Serenade--F, Op 95.  Strs & Winds. . . . . . . . . . Andraud
STRAUSS  Suite for W. W. --Bb, Op 4.  2Fl, 2Ob, 2Cl, 3Bn, 4Hn. . . . . . Leuckart(1911)
        Serenade--Eb, Op 7.  Double WWQuar, 4Hn, CBn(Tuba). . . . UE(1884); Andraud

# BIBLIOGRAPHY

Altmann, Wilhelm. Kammermusik-Katalog (Rev. ed; Leipzig: Breitkopf & Hartel, 1945).

Carter, Elliott. "Walter Piston," in MQ, XXXII (1946) 354-375.

Cobbett, Walter Willson. Cobbett's Cyclopedic Survey of Chamber Music (London: Oxford University Press, 1929). 2 vol. In addition to the list of compositions alphabetically by composer, there are articles under names of instruments and countries.

Dictionnaire Biographique Francais Contemporain (Paris: Centre International de Documentation, 1950).

Einstein, Alfred. Mozart, His Character, His Work, tr. by Arthur Mendel and Nathan Broder (N. Y.: Oxford University Press, 1945).

Einstein, Alfred, ed. Chronologisch-thematisches Verzeichnis ... Mozarts, von Dr. L. R. von Köchel (3rd ed.; Ann Arbor: J. W. Edwards, 1947).

Eitner, Robert. Biographisch-Bibliographisches Quellen-Lexikon (reprint; N. Y.: Musurgia).

Evans, Edwin. Chamber and Orchestral Music of Johannes Brahms (London: Reeves, 1933-34). 2 vol.

Ewen, David. American Composers Today (N. Y.: H. W. Wilson Co., 1949).

Ewen, David. Living Musicians (N. Y.: H. W. Wilson Co., 1940).

The Edwin A. Fleisher Music Collection in the Free Library of Philadelphia (Philadelphia: privately printed by press of Edward Stern and Co., 1933).

Foster, Levin Wilson. A Directory of Clarinet Music (Pittsfield, Mass.: A. E. Johnson, 1940).

Glanville-Hicks, P. "Virgil Thomson," in MQ, XXXV (1949) 209-225.

Goldman, Richard F. "The Music of Wallingford Riegger," in MQ, XXXVI (1950) 39-61.

Grove, Sir George. Grove's Dictionary of Music and Musicians, ed. by H. C. Colles (3rd ed.; N. Y.: Macmillan, 1937). 5 vol. Supplementary Volume, ed. by Colles (N. Y.: Macmillan, 1940). 1 vol.

Howard, John Tasker. Our American Music (3rd ed.; N. Y.: Thomas Y. Crowell, 1946).

Howard, John Tasker. Our Contemporary Composers (N. Y.: Thomas Y. Crowell, 1942).

King, Robert, ed. Music for Brass (North Easton, Mass., 1952 [1951]).

The Macmillan Encyclopedia of Music and Musicians, comp. and ed. by Albert E. Wier (N. Y.: Macmillan, 1938). Not always reliable.

Mazzeo, Rosario. A Brief Survey of Chamber Music (2nd ed.; Boston: Cundy-Bettoney Co., Inc., 1938).

McArdle, Donald W.    "A Check List of Beethoven's Chamber Music," Music and Letters,
    XXVII (1946) 44-59, 83-101, 156-174.

McNamara, Daniel I., ed.    The ASCAP Biographical Dictionary of Composers, Authors, and
    Publishers (N.Y.: Thomas Y. Crowell, 1948).

N.A.S.M.    Solo Literature for Wind Instruments   (Bulletin of the National Association of
    Schools of Music #31, Jan. 1951).   In spite of the title, there are numerous ensemble
    listings.

Reis, Claire R.    Composers in America (rev. ed.; N.Y.: Macmillan, 1947).

Riemann, Hugo.    Musik-Lexikon, ed. by A. Einstein (10th ed.; Berlin: Max Hesses Verlag,
    1922).

Russell, Myron E., chairman.    Catalog of Woodwind Choir Literature (Compiled by College
    Band Directors National Assn., Mimeograph, 1949).   A group project, some inconsist-
    ency of symbols, typographical and real errors, but a valuable list with considerable
    material.

School Music Competition-Festivals Manual (Chicago: The National School Band, Orchestra
    and Vocal Associations, 1942).   Primarily concerned with teaching material of course,
    but in addition has sections devoted to publishers' addresses, etc.

Slonimsky, Nicolas.    "Roy Harris," in MQ, XXXIII (1947) 17-37.

S.P.A.M.    Society for the Publication of American Music, issue of chamber music listed in
    MQ, XXXVI#1 (Jan., 1950), advertisement on last page.   Information and their music
    can be supplied by G. Schirmer.

Thompson, Oscar, ed.    The International Cyclopedia of Music and Musicians, rev. and en-
    larged by Nicolas Slonimsky (5th ed.; N.Y.: Dodd, Mead and Co., 1949).

Tuthill, Burnet C.    "Clarinet Bibliography," Woodwind Magazine, II#8 (Apr., 1950) 12, 14.
    Commentary on each item.

Tuthill, Burnet C.    "Daniel Gregory Mason," in MQ, XXXIV (1948) 46-60.

# ABBREVIATIONS AND SYMBOLS

## Instruments

| | | | | |
|---|---|---|---|---|
| AltCl | Alto Clarinet | | Gamba | Viola da Gamba |
| AltFl | Alto Flute | | Hn | French Horn |
| AltSx | Alto Saxophone | | Hp | Harp |
| Bar | Baritone (Horn) | | Hpschd | Harpsichord |
| BarSx | Baritone Saxophone | | Ob | Oboe |
| Bn | Bassoon | | Perc | Percussion |
| BsCl | Bass Clarinet | | Pf | Pianoforte |
| BsFl | Bass Flute | | Picc | Piccolo |
| BsSx | Bass Saxophone | | SopSx | Soprano Saxophone |
| Cb | Contrabass, String Bass | | Sx | Saxophone |
| CBn | Contrabassoon | | Tb | Trombone |
| Cl | (1) Bb or A Sopr. Clarinet | | TenHn | European Tenor Horn |
| | (2) Clarinet family | | TenSx | Tenor Saxophone |
| Ct | Cornet | | Tt | Trumpet |
| Dr | Drum | | Tuba | Tuba |
| EH | English Horn | | Va | Viola |
| Fl | Flute | | Vc | Violoncello |
| | | | Vl | Violin |

## Others

| | | | | |
|---|---|---|---|---|
| Quar | Quartet | | Op | Opus |
| Quint | Quintet | | --G | Key, G major in this case |
| WW | Woodwind | | --g· | Key, g minor in this case |
| WWQuar | Fl, Ob, Cl, Bn | | C | Contra |
| WWQuint | WWQuar, Hn | | Bs | (1) bass instrument |
| ClQuar | 2Cl, AltCl, BsCl | | | (2) bass line, e. g. Vc & Cb |
| SxQuar | 2AltSx, TenSx, BarSx | | FigBs | Baroque Figured Bass |
| Str | String or Strings | | Arr: | Arranged for or by |
| StrQuar | 2Vl, Va, Vc | | Arr. | Arrangement |
| StrQuint | 2Vl, Va, Vc, Cb | | Ed: | Edited for or by |
| | | | Ed. | Edition |

## SYMBOLS AND INFORMATION ON PUBLISHERS

### Symbol

Alfred    Alfred Music Co. , Inc. , 145 W. 45th St, N. Y.
       American Music Center, 250 W. 57th St. , N. Y. 19. Established to promote interest in American composers; handles editions of Arrow Press, Cos Cob Press, New Music Edition music and recordings, and has on file for general inspection a great number of manuscripts of many young composers.
       Amphion Edit.    See: E-V
Andraud    Albert J. Andraud, 2871 Erie St. , Cincinnati 8. A most complete library of wind music, both domestic and foreign.
Arrow    Arrow Music Press, Inc. See: American Music Center.

AMP         Associated Music Publishers, Inc., 25 W. 45th St., N.Y. 19. Agents for:
           Belaiev (Paris), Bote & Bock (Berlin), Breitkopf & Härtel (Leipzig), Broadcast
           Music (N.Y. & Canada), Doblinger (Vienna), Eschig (Paris), Hainauer (London),
           ? Kahnt (Leipzig), ? Leuckart (Leipzig), Nagel (Hannover), Philharmonia
           (Vienna), Russian-Amer. Mus. Publ. (N.Y.), Schott (London & Mainz), Simrock
           (Leipzig), Thomas-Cole (N.Y.), and their own publications.

Augener    Augener. See ECSch.

MBaron     M. Baron Co., 8 W. 45th St., N.Y. 19. Agents for: Carisch (Milan), J. & W.
           Chester (London), Edit. Decruck (Paris), Enoch (Paris), Hamelle (Paris),
           Leduc (Paris), Edit. Noel (Paris), Edit. Schott Freres (Brussels), Edit.
           Musicales Sellmer (Paris), Skandinavisk Musikforlag (Copenhagen), Union
           Musical Espanola (Madrid), and others.

B-N         Baxter-Northrup, now Keynote Music Service. See: Keynote.

Belaiev    Belaiev, Paris. See: AMP

Belwin     Belwin, Inc., Rockville Centre, Long Island, N.Y. Agent for Bosworth & Co. Has
           an excellent and carefully prepared catalog, particularly useful in selecting
           teaching material.

Boosey     Boosey & Hawkes, Box 418, Lynbrook, Long Island, N.Y.

Boston     Boston Music Co., 116 Boylston St., Boston. General dealer.
           Bosworth & Co. See: Belwin.
           Bote & Bock, Berlin. See: AMP

B&H        Breitkopf & Hartel, Leipzig. See: AMP

Broadcast  Broadcast Music Inc., N.Y. & Canada. See: AMP

Broude    Broude Bros., 56 W. 45th St., N.Y. 19.

Carisch    S.A. Carisch, Milan. See: MBaron.

Chester    J. & W. Chester, England. ECSch, MBaron are dealers.

CompPr    The Composers Press, 853 7th Ave., N.Y.

CosCob    The Cos Cob Press. See: American Music Center.
           Costallat & Cie, Paris. See: MBaron.
           A. Cranz, Brussels. Exclusive agent: SMPC.

C-B         Cundy-Bettoney Co., Inc., Bradlee & Madison, Hyde Park 36, Boston.

Curwen    J. Curwen & Sons. See: GSch.

Decruck    Maurice Decruck, Paris. See: MBaron.
           H. Deiss. See: E-V
           Doblinger, Vienna. See: AMP.

Durand     Durand, France. See: E-V.
           Edition Musicus. See: MBaron.

Edit. Coop.   Editorial Cooperativa Interamericana. Exclusive agent: SMPC.

EMB        Educational Music Bureau, 30 E. Adams, Chicago. Handles the music of practic-
           ally all domestic publishers.

E-V         Elkan-Vogel, Inc., 1712 Sansom St., Philadelphia 3. Agents for: Durand, Jobert,
           Lemoine, Herelle, Amphion, Sirene Musical, Lerolle, H. Deiss, Senart.
           Enoch & Cie., Paris. Exclusive agent: SMPC; MBaron a dealer.

Eschig     Eschig, Paris. See: AMP.

CFisch     Carl Fischer, Inc., 56-62 Cooper Square, N.Y. 3. Agent: OUP.
           Francis, Day, & Hunter, London. See: Mills.

Gamble    Gamble Hinge, 218 S. Wabash, Chicago 5.
           Hainauer, London. See: AMP.

Hamelle    J. Hamelle, Paris. Agent: MBaron.

Hansen    Wilhelm Hansen, Copenhagen. See: AMP.
           Harms, N.Y. See: MPHC.
           Herelle, France. See: E-V.

Heugel     Heugel & Cie., Paris. See: Merc.

IMC        International Music Co., 509 5th Ave., N.Y. 17. Good listings.
           Jobert, France. See: E-V.

Kahnt     Kahnt, Leipzig. See: ? AMP.

Keynote    Keynote Music Service (the old Baxter-Northrup), 837 S. Olive, Los Angeles. The
           well known general dealers of the West.

Kjos        Neil A. Kjos Music Co. , 223 W. Lake, Chicago.
Leduc       Alphonse Leduc & Cie. , Paris.  See: MBaron.
Leeds       Leeds Music Corp. , RKO Bldg. , Radio City, N. Y. 20.  Dealers of Russian music.
            Legouix, Paris.  Dealer: MBaron.
Lemoine     Lemoine & Cie. , France.  See: E-V.
            Alfred Lengnick, London.  See: Mills.
            Lerolle & Cie.  See: E-V.
            F. E. C. Leuckart, Leipzig.  See: AMP.
Marks       Edward B. Marks Music Corp. , 1250 6th Ave. , Radio City, N. Y. 20.
McG & M     McGinnis & Marx, 408 2nd Ave. , N. Y.  Publishers, dealers, importers.
Merc        Mercury Music Co. , 47 W. 63rd St. , N. Y. 23.  Agents: Heugel (Paris), Music
                Press (N. Y. ).
Mills       Mills Music Inc. , 1619 Broadway, N. Y. 19.  Agents: Alfred Lengnick (London),
                Francis, Day, & Hunter (London).
MusExc      The Music Exchange, 109 W. 48th St. , N. Y. 19.  Foreign and domestic.
Mus f Brass Music For Brass, 7 Canton St. , North Easton, Mass.  Absolutely the finest
                catalog of brass music, a model of scholarly presentation of music for sale.
MusPr       Music Press, Inc.  See: Merc.
MPHC        Music Publ. Holding Corp. , 488 Madison Ave. , N. Y.  Agents: Witmark, Harms,
                Remick.
Nagel       Nagel, Hannover.  See:  AMP.
NME         New Music Edition.   See:  American Music Center.
            P. Noel, Paris.  Dealer: MBaron.
            Novello, England.  Dealer: ECSch.
OUP         Oxford Univ. Press, Music Dept. , 36 Soho Sq. , London W. 1.  See: ECSch.
Peters      C. F. Peters Corp. , 1209 Carnegie Hall, 881 7th Ave. , N. Y. 19.  Also: UE.
            Philharmonia, Vienna.  See: AMP.
Presser     Theodore Presser Co. , Bryn Mawr, Pa.
Remick      Remick.  See:  MPHC.
Ricordi     G. Ricordi & Co. , 1270 Ave. of the Americas, N. Y. 20.  Represent the European
                Ricordi, although at present they have no catalog of same.
Rubank      Rubank, Inc. , 5544 W. Armstrong Ave. , Chicago 30.  Mostly teaching material.
            Russian-Amer.  Music Publishers, N. Y.  See: AMP.
ECSch       E. C. Schirmer, 221 Columbus Ave. , Boston 16.  Dealer for: Peters, AMP, OUP,
                GSch, Mus f Brass, and general.
GSch        G. Schirmer, 3 E. 43rd St. , N. Y. 17.  Agents: Curwen, Hanson Edit. , SPAM.
Schott      Schott, London & Mainz.  See:  AMP.
            Edit. Schott Freres, Brussels.  See:  MBaron.
            Edit. Musicales Sellmer, Paris.   See: MBaron.
Senart      M. Senart.   See: E-V.
Simrock     Simrock, Leipzig.  See: AMP.
SireneM     La Sirene Musicale.   See: E-V.
            Skandinavisk  Musikforlag, Copenhagen.  See: MBaron.
SPAM        Society for the Publication of American Music, Box 269, Wall St. Station, N. Y. 5.
                See:  GSch.
SMPC        Southern Music Publishing Co. , Inc. , 1619 Broadway, N. Y. 19.  Exclusive agent:
                Cranz (Brussels), Enoch (Paris), Edit. Coop. (S. Amer. ), other S. American
                music.
Spratt      Jack Spratt, 21-23 West End Ave. , Old Greenwich, Conn.
            Stainer & Bell, England.  See: ECSch.
            Thomas-Cole, N. Y.  See: AMP.
            Union Musical Espanola, Madrid.  See: MBaron.
UE          Universal Edition, Vienna.   Now handled by Peters.
Valley      Valley Music Press, Sage Hall, Smith College, Northampton, Mass.
Witmark     Witmark & Sons.  See:  MPHC.

82